# WELSH XXX JOKES

ISBN: 0 86243 724 5

Printed and published in Wales
by Y Lolfa Cyf., Talybont, Ceredigion SY24 5AP
*e-mail* ylolfa@ylolfa.com
*website* www.ylolfa.com
*tel.* (01970) 832 304
*fax* 832 782

# contents

# brats XXX

Jack invited his mother over for dinner. During the meal, his mother couldn't help noticing how beautiful Jack's room-mate Mair was. She had long been suspicious of a relationship between Jack and his room-mate, and this only made her more curious.

Over the course of the evening, while watching the two interact, she started to wonder if there was more between Jack and the room-mate than met the eye. Reading his mother's thoughts, Jack volunteered, "I know what you must be thinking, but I assure you, Mair and I are just room-mates."

About a week later, Mair came to Jack and said, "Ever since your mother came to dinner, I've been unable to find the beautiful silver gravy ladle. You don't suppose she took it, do you?" Jack said, "Well, I doubt it, but I'll write her a letter just to be sure." So he sat down and wrote: "Dear Mam, I'm not saying you did take a gravy ladle from my house, and I'm not saying you did not take a gravy ladle. But the fact remains that one has been missing ever since you were here for dinner."

Several days later, Jack received a letter from his mother which read: "Dear Jack, I'm not saying that you do sleep with Mair, and I'm not saying that you do not sleep with Mair. But the fact remains that if she was sleeping in her own bed, she would have found the gravy ladle by now. Love, Mam."

x  x  x

Gareth was in the habit of sucking his thumb all the time. His mother tried everything to break him of the habit. Finally, one day she pointed to a fat man with a very large stomach and said that the man's stomach had grown because he did not stop sucking his thumb. The next day, Gareth was with his mother in a supermarket in Swansea, and he kept staring at a woman with a stomach that was obviously not normal. In fact the woman was very pregnant. Finally the irate woman said to Gareth, "Stop staring at me like that! You don't know who I am."

"No," replied Gareth, "but I do know what you have been doing."

x  x  x

Tudur bach goes to school, and Miss Roberts says, "Today we're going to learn multi-syllable words, class. Does anyone have an example for me?" Tudur bach waves his hand, "Me, miss, me, me!" Miss Roberts says, "Right-o, Tudur, what's your multi-syllable word?" Tudur bach says, "Mas-tur-bate." Miss Roberts says, "Duw duw, Tudur, that's quite a mouthful!" Tudur bach replies, "No, miss – you're thinking of a blow job. I'm talking about a wank."

x  x  x

Miss Morgan asked the class to use 'absolutely' in a sentence. Sian raised her hand and said the sky is absolutely blue. The teacher said no, that was incorrect – sometimes it was black or had other colours. Another little lad raised his hand and said, "The leaves on the trees are absolutely green." Teacher said the leaves could be other colours at different times of year. Tomi raised his hand and asked if there were lumps in farts. The teacher said she didn't believe there were. Tomi said, "Well, in that case, Miss Morgan, I absolutely just shit in my pants!"

x   x   x

Meirion walked into his dad's bedroom one day, only to catch him sitting on the side of his bed, sliding a condom on. Meirion's father, in an attempt to hide his full erection with a condom on it, bent over as if to look under the bed.

"What are you doing, Daddy?" Meirion asked curiously. His dad quickly replied, "I thought I saw a mouse go underneath the bed," to which Meirion replied, "What are you going to do – ***k it?"

x   x   x

Two young boys were spending the night at their grandparents. At bedtime, the two boys knelt beside their beds to say their prayers when the youngest one began praying at the top of his lungs. "I PRAY FOR A NEW BICYCLE... I PRAY FOR A NEW GAMEBOY... I PRAY FOR A NEW DVD..."

His older brother leaned over and nudged the

younger brother and said, "Why are you shouting your prayers? God isn't deaf." To which the little brother replied, "No, but Grandma is!"

x  x  x

Young Dilwyn comes home from school one day and is met at the door by his granny, who asks what he learned in school today. He replied, "We learned about sex." His granny just stands there, almost in shock. Later that day, she tells his mam about their conversation. Dilwyn's mam says, "Gran, sex is a regularly studied subject in school these days."

Later that evening, granny walks past Dilwyn's room, sees him vigorously masturbating, and says to him, "After you finish your homework, come down for dinner."

x  x  x

Little Ifan and Meryl are playing in a sandpit. Ifan has to go to have a pee, and he has been told by his mam to always be polite and not talk about private matters in public. At first, Ifan holds it in for a little while, because he does not know what to say to Meryl to excuse himself. Then he remembers what his Mam had said at the restaurant to excuse herself from the table. So he turns to Meryl and says, "Will you excuse me? I have to go and powder my nose." And saying that, Ifan jumps out of the sandbox and rushes to the loo. When he comes back, Meryl looks up at him and asks "Did you powder your nose?"

"Yes," said Ifan stepping back into the sandpit.

"Well then," says Meryl, "You'd better close your purse, because your lipstick is hanging out!"

x  x  x

Little Tommy had a swearing problem, and his dad was getting tired of it. He decided to ask his doctor what to do. His doctor advised him that as it was December, he should ask Tommy what he wanted from Father Christmas. If Tommy swore, his father should leave a pile of dog muck in place of the gift.

Two days before Christmas, his father asked Tommy what he wanted for Christmas. Tommy replied, "I want a bloody teddy-bear laying right bloody here beside me when I wake up on Christmas morning. Then, when I go downstairs, I want to see a blasted train going around the bloody Christmas tree, and when I go outside I want to see a bloody red and white bike leaning up against the damn garage!"

Christmas morning, little Tommy woke up and rolled over into a big pile of dog muck. Confused, he walked downstairs and saw a load of dog muck around the Christmas tree. Scratching his head, he walked outside and saw a huge pile of dog muck by the garage. He walked back inside with a curious look on his face.

His dad smiled and asked... "So Tommy, what did Santa bring you this year?"

Tommy replied, "I think I got a dog, but I can't find the ****ing thing."

x  x  x

At a Rhondda Primary shool, Miss Dilwyns asked her class to make a sentence using the word 'fascinate'. Rhiannon puts up her hand and said, "I went to the exhibition in Cardiff last Saturday and saw the dinosaurs and was really fascinated."

"That's good," said Miss Dilwyns, "but I want the word 'fascinate'."

Mari raised her hand and said, "Please Miss, I went to Bristol Zoo last summer, and I was really fascinated."

"Yes, Mari," said Miss Dilwyns, "but can someone give me a sentence with just the word 'fascinate' in it."

Jack bach puts his hand up and says, "Please Miss, my sister has got a coat with nine buttons on it, but she can only fasten eight, because she's got big tits."

x  x  x

Little Tommy was in the garden filling in a hole when his neighbour peered over the fence. Interested in what the cheeky-faced youngster was doing, he politely asked, "What are you up to there, Tommy?"

"Well, my goldfish died," replied Tommy tearfully, without looking up, "and I've just buried him." The neighbour was concerned: "That's an awfully big hole for a goldfish, isn't it?" Tommy patted down the last heap of earth then replied, "That's because he's inside your ****ing cat!"

x  x  x

Ianto wanted to purchase a gift for Betsan, his new sweetheart, on her birthday, and as they had not been dating very long, after careful thought, he decided a pair of gloves would be ideal; romantic, but not too personal. Accompanied by his sweetheart's younger sister Sian, he went to Marks and bought a pair of white gloves. Sian bought some panties for herself. During the packing, the shop assistant mixed up the items and Sian got the gloves and the Ianto's dearest Betsan got the panties. Without checking the contents, Ianto proudly sealed the parcel and sent it to Betsan with the note :

"My darling Betsan,

I chose these because I noticed that you are not in the habit of wearing any when we go out in the evening. If it had not been for your sister Sian, I would have chosen the long ones with the buttons, but she suggested the short ones are easier to remove. These are a delicate shade, but the lady I bought them from showed me the pair she had been wearing for the past three weeks and they were hardly soiled. I had her try yours on for me and she looked really smart. I wish I was there so that I could put them on for you the first time, as no doubt other hands will come in contact with them before I have a chance to see you again. When you take them off, remember to blow in them before putting them away as they will naturally be a little damp from wearing. Just think how many times I will kiss them during the coming year. I hope you will wear them for me on Friday night.

All my love
        Ianto


PS The latest style is to wear them folded down with a little fur showing."

x x x

One day, Jimmy is walking home from school. When he gets home, he finds his grandpa sitting in the back garden without any trousers on.

"Grandpa, do you realize that you're not wearing any trousers?" he says to his grandpa.

"Yes, Jimmy, I do," his grandpa replies. Jimmy then says, "Well, why are you outside without any trousers on, Grandpa?"

His grandpa looks at Jimmy and responds, "Well, Jimmy, yesterday I sat outside without a shirt for too long, and I got a stiff neck. This was your grandma's idea."

x x x

Young Aled goes into a chemist's to buy condoms. The chemist says the condoms come in packs of 3, 9 or 12 and asks Aled which pack he wants.

"Well," Aled replies, "I've been seeing this girl for a few weeks and she's really hot. I want the condoms because I think tonight's the night. We're having dinner with her parents, and then we're going out for a few drinks and afterwards I'm going to give her one. Once she's had me, she'll want me all the time, so you'd better give me the 12 pack." Aled pays for the pack and leaves.

Later that evening, Aled sits down to dinner with his girlfriend and her parents. He asks if he might give the blessing, and they agree. He begins the prayer, and continues praying for several minutes. His girlfriend leans over and says, "You never told me that you were such a religious person, Aled."

He leans over to her and says, "You never told me that your dad is a chemist!"

x  x  x

Two lads from Corris were walking home from Machynlleth one summer evening when they came across a sheep stuck in the hedge.

"Bloody hell," said Dylan. "I wish that was Madonna stuck there!"

"Sod that," replied Iwan. "I wish it was dark!"

x  x  x

Tommy is in school working on his arithmetic. The teacher says, "Imagine there are five blackbirds sitting on a fence. You pick up your airgun and shoot one. How many blackbirds are left?"

Tommy thinks for a moment and says, "None!" The teacher replies, "None? How do you work that out?" The little boy says, "If I shoot one, all the other birds will fly away scared, leaving none on the fence." The teacher replies, "Hmm, not exactly, but I do like the way you think!"

Tommy then says, "Teacher, let me ask you a question. There are three women sitting on a park bench, eating ice cream cones. One is licking her cone, another is biting it and the third one is sucking it. How can you tell which one of the women is married?"

The teacher ponders the question uncomfortably and then finally replies, "Well, I guess the one sucking her cone."

To which Tommy replies, "Actually, it's the one with the wedding ring, but I do like the way YOU think!"

# ωomen XXX

Blodwen went to the Doctor and complained that she was always tired.

"Well, Blodwen," said the doctor, "I'm afraid you'll have to cut down on your sex life. How often do you have sex now?"

"Oh," replied Blodwen, "three times a week. Mondays, Wednesdays and Fridays."

"Well," said the doctor, "can I suggest you cut out Wednesdays?"

"Oh!" said a horrified Blodwen, "I couldn't do that! It's the only night I'm at home with my husband!"

x   x   x

Myfanwy took her daughter to the doctor and asked him to give her an examination to determine the cause of her daughter's swollen abdomen. It only took the doctor about two seconds to say, "Your daughter is pregnant."

Myfanwy turned red with fury and she argued with the doctor that her daughter was a good girl and would never compromise her reputation by having sex with a boy. The doctor faced the window and silently looked out at the horizon. Myfanwy became enraged and screamed, "Stop looking out the window! Aren't you paying attention to me?"

"Yes, of course I'm paying attention, Mrs Jones. It's just that the last time this happened, a star appeared in the East, and three wise men came. If they show up again, I'd like to witness it!"

x   x   x

Three nurses go into the morgue, and there's Dai, lying dead there, with an erection.

The first nurse sees it, says, "I'm gagging for it," gets on top of Dai, and has her way with him. The second nurse says, "Aye, so am I, shame to let it go to waste," and she does the same. They turn to the third nurse and ask her if she is having a go. She replies that she is having her period, and declines. One of the nurses reply, "Dai's dead anyway – he'll not be bothered." The last nurse agrees with this, gets on and does her thing too. Just after she finishes, Dai sits up. The nurses ask him, "We thought you were dead!" and Dai replies, "After two jump starts and a blood transfusion, you wouldn't be dead either!"

x   x   x

Myfanwy came home and told her mother that her boyfriend had proposed but she had turned him down because she found out he was an atheist, and didn't believe in heaven or hell.

"Marry him anyway, dear," the mother said. "Between the two of us, we'll show him just how wrong he is."

x   x   x

Two nuns riding down a cobbled road on bicycles. First one says to the other, "I've never come this way before."

Other nun says, "Neither have I. It's probably the cobbles."

x   x   x

An elderly gentleman calls his friend Nia and announces, "For my 80th birthday, I'm going to get one of those 20-year-olds." Nia responds by saying "So, my birthday is next week and I'm going to get a 20-year-old, too."

"What's the difference?" Dai asks.

"20 goes into 80 a lot more than 80 goes into 20!"

x   x   x

A guy goes to visit his grandmother and he brings his friends with him. While he's talking to his grandmother, his friend starts eating the peanuts on the coffee table, and finishes them off. As they're leaving, his friend says to his grandmother, "Thanks for the peanuts."

She says, "Yes, since I lost my dentures I can only suck the chocolate off them."

x   x   x

Young Marged goes into the doctor's office for a checkup. As she takes off her blouse, he notices a red 'C' on her chest.

"How did you get that mark on your chest?" asks the doctor.

"Oh, my boyfriend went to Cambridge and he's so proud of it that he never takes off his Camebridge sweatshirt, even when we make love," she replies.

A couple of days later, Susan comes in for a checkup. As she takes off her blouse, he notices a blue 'O' on her chest.

"How did you get that mark on your chest?" asks the doctor.

"Oh, my boyfriend went to Oxford and he's so proud of it that he never takes off his Oxford sweatshirt, even when we make love," she replies.

A couple of days later, Mary comes in for a checkup. As she takes off her blouse, he notices a green 'M' on her chest.

"Do you have a boyfriend at Manchester?" asks the doctor.

"No, at Wessex. Why do you ask?"

x   x   x

Nia was worried that her husband was losing interest in her sexually. She went out and bought some very sexy lingerie, complete with crotchless panties. She posed in bed and awaited his arrival. When he came into the bedroom, she threw the sheets back, spread her legs, and said, "Welcome home, cariad. Do you want some of this?"

With a horrified look on his face, he replied, "Iesu mawr, no! Look what it did to your underwear!"

x   x   x

Sion asked his wife if she fancied anything out of the Kama Sutra. Anwen said, "No cariad, I'm not all that keen on Indian takeaways!"

x   x   x

Iwan said to his wife, "Let's go out tonight, have some fun, and paint the town red."

"Aye," replied his wife, "but if you get home before me, please leave the kitchen light on, cariad."

x   x   x

Julie walks into a chemist's shop in Aber and asks young Jack behind the counter if they sell extra-large condoms. Jack looks at Julie quizzically, but shrugs and says "Yes, we do. They're right here behind the counter."

Julie thanks Jack and stands there... and stands there... and stands there.

Jack eventually asks Julie, "Is there something else I can help you with, Madam?" Julie smiles sweetly at Jack and says, "No, thank you, cariad. I'm just waiting here to see who buys them!"

x   x   x

The day after it was supposed to have snowed but didn't, a Welsh female weather reader turned to the weatherman and asked, "So Ianto, where's that eight inches you promised me last night?"

x x x

Blodwen was a 90-year-old recently bereaved woman who simply couldn't come to terms with the loss of her dearest Ephraim, and decided to join him in death. She thought it best to get things over with quickly and dug out Ephraim's 16-bore and decided to shoot herself in the heart, which was deeply broken. So as not to miss the vital organ, she aimed it under her left breast and pulled the trigger. Later that evening, Blodwen was admitted to hospital with gunshot wounds to her knee.

x x x

On a long international flight, one of the plane's wings is struck by lightning. Myfanwy panics. Screaming, she stands up in the front of the plane. 'I'm too young to die!' she wails. Then she yells, "Well, if I'm going to die, I want my last minutes on earth to be memorable! I've had plenty of excitement in my life, but no-one has ever made me really feel like a woman! Well, I've had it! Is there ANYONE on this plane who can make me feel like a WOMAN?" For a moment there is silence. Everyone has forgotten their own peril, and they all stare, rivetted, at the desperate creature in the front of the plane. Then, Ianto stands up in the rear of the plane.

"I can make you feel like a woman," he says. He's handsome, tall, well-built, with long blonde hair and blue eyes. He starts to walk slowly up the aisle, unbuttoning his shirt, one button at a time. No-one moves.

Myfanwy is breathing heavily in anticipation as the man approaches. He removes his shirt. Muscles ripple across his chest. As he reaches Myfanwy, and extends the arm holding his shirt to the trembling woman, he whispers: "Cariad, iron this."

Ianto walks into the Red Lion after quarrelling with his wife, and has one too many to drink. He looks over into the corner and notices a beautiful lady sitting down. He turns to her and says, "Hey how about it, you and me, getting together? I've got a couple of quid and it looks like you could do with a little hard cash." She stands up and says, "Ianto, what makes you think I charge by the inch?"

x   x   x

Dai came home from the pub one night after work, when Mari asked him, "Can I have some money? I want to buy a bra." Dai replied, "What for? You've got nothing to put in it!" Mari said, "You wear pants, don't you?"

x   x   x

Geraint: Shall we try a different position tonight?
Myfanwy: Good idea. You stand by the ironing board while I sit on the sofa, watch telly and fart.

x   x   x

Researcher: Excuse me madam, I'm conducting a survey.

Woman: Yes, what is it about?

Researcher: We're asking people what they think about sex on the television...

Woman: Very uncomfortable, I would imagine!

x    x    x

A young, attractive woman thought she might have some fun with a stiff-looking military man at a cocktail party, so she walked over and asked him, "Major, when was the last time you had sex?"

"1956," was his reply.

"No wonder you look so uptight!" she exclaimed. "Major, you need to get out more!"

"I'm not sure I understand you," he answered, glancing at his watch. "It's only 2014 now."

x    x    x

Annie, Blodwen, Mari and Myfanwy were sitting in the café discussing their comedowns. Annie says, "Girls, we've known each other for ages, but I have a confession to make, I've got to get it off my chest. I'm a kleptomaniac, but don't worry, I've never stolen anything from any of my friends and never will."

"Well," says Blodwen, "I may as well confess, I must tell you all, I'm a nymphomaniac, but, don't worry, I'd never try it on with any of your husbands."

Mari said, "Well, I've also got a confession to make, I'm a lesbian, but not to worry, none of you are my type."

Myfanwy turned to the others and said, "I also must confess, I'm an incredible gossip, and if you excuse me for a minute, I've got a few phone calls to make!"

x   x   x

A blonde is walking down Cambrian street with her blouse open and her right breast hanging out. Young Geraint approaches her and says, "Excuse me Miss, are you aware that I could report you for indecent exposure?" She says, "Why?"

"Because your right breast is hanging out."

She looks down and says, "Oh ***k it! I left the baby on the train again!"

x   x   x

At a crowded bus stop in Cardiff Central a beautiful young woman was waiting for the bus. Dressed up for work, she was wearing a very tight mini skirt. As the bus rolled up and it became her turn to get on the bus, she became aware that her skirt was too tight to allow her leg to come up to the height of the first step.

So slightly embarrassed and with a quick smile to the bus driver she reached behind her and unzipped her skirt a little thinking that this would give her enough slack to raise her leg.

Again she tried to make the step onto the bus to discover she still could not make the step. So, a little more embarrassed she once again reached behind her and unzipped her skirt a little more. And for a second time she attempted the step and once again, much to her disgust she could not raise her leg because of the tight skirt.

So with a coy little smile to the impatient driver she again unzipped the offending skirt to give a little more slack and again was unable to make the step.

About this time, Ianto, who was behind her in the queue, picked her up easily from the waist and placed her lightly on the step of the bus.

Well, she went ballistic and turned on the would-be hero, screeching at him "How dare you touch my body! I don't even know you!"

At this Ianto said, "Well cariad, normally I'd agree with you, but after you unzipped my fly three times, I sort of thought we might be friends."

x   x   x

Two women went out one weekend without their husbands. As they walked home at dawn, both of them drunk, they felt the urge to pee.

They noticed the only place to stop was a cemetery. Scared and drunk, they stopped and decided to go there anyway. The first one did not have anything to clean herself with, so she took off her panties and used them to clean herself and discarded them. The second, not finding anything either, thought "I'm not getting rid of my panties," so she used the ribbon of a flower wreath to clean herself.

The morning after, the two husbands were talking to each other on the phone, and one says to the other: "We have to be on the look-out. It seems that these two were up to no good last night. My wife came home without her panties." The other one responded:

"You're lucky! Mine came home with a card stuck to her ass that read, 'We will never forget you'".

x x x

Blodwen goes to the South Wales Mail and enquires about placing an advert in the lonely hearts column.

"Certainly," said the assistant. "That's £1 per insertion."

"Is that all?" replied Blodwen. "Forget the advert – I'll have £20's worth."

x x x

Jack: Since I first laid eyes on you, I've wanted to make love to you in the worst way.
Marged: Well, you succeeded.

x x x

Frank: Two inches more, and I would be king.
Myfanwy: Two inches less, and you'd be queen.

x x x

Mari accompanied her husband Ianto to the doctor's surgery. After his checkup, the doctor called Mari into his office alone. He said, "Ianto is suffering from a very severe disease, combined with horrible stress. If you don't do the following, Ianto will surely die. Each morning, fix him a healthy breakfast. Be pleasant, and make sure he is in a good mood. For lunch make him a nutritious meal. For dinner prepare an especially nice meal for him. Don't burden him with housework, as he probably has had a hard day. Don't discuss your problems with him, it will only make his stress worse. And most importantly, make love with your husband several times a week and satisfy his every whim. If you can do this for the next 10 months to a year, I think Ianto will be a new man and will regain his health completely."

On the way home, Ianto asked Mari, "What did the doctor say?"

"You're going to die."

x   x   x

Blodwen, who was by now getting on in age, goes to the doctor and asks his help to revive her husband's sex drive.

"What about trying Viagra?" asks the doctor.

"Not a chance," says Blodwen. "He won't even take an aspirin for a headache."

"No problem," replies the doctor. "Drop it into his coffee; he won't even taste it. Try it and come back in a week to let me know how you got on."

A week later our Blodwen returns to the doctor and he inquires as to how things went.

"Oh it was terrible, just terrible, doctor."

"What happened?" asks the doctor.

"Well, I did as you advised and slipped it in his coffee. The effect was immediate. He jumped straight up, swept the cutlery off the table, at the same time ripping my clothes off, and then he proceeded to make passionate love to me on the tabletop. It was terrible."

"What was terrible?" said the doctor. "Was the sex not good?"

"Oh, no doctor, the sex was the best I've had in 25 years, but I'll never be able to show my face in McDonald's again."

x  x  x

Three old ladies are sitting in the park on a beautiful spring day, feeding the pigeons and the squirrels, when suddenly, a man in a long trench coat jumps in front of them and throws open his coat. He's completely naked under his coat. The three old ladies haven't seen such a thing in a very long time, and their blood pressure shoots up quickly. The first old lady lets out a gasp and has a stroke. The second old lady sees this and it's too much for her – she gasps and has a stroke, too. The third old lady doesn't have a stroke – she's sitting too far away and can't reach.

x  x  x

Megan was in bed with her lover, Ianto, when she heard her Dai opening the front door.

"Hurry!" she said. "Stand in the corner." She quickly rubbed baby oil all over him and then dusted him with talcum powder. "Don't move until I tell you to," she whispered. "Just pretend you're a statue."

"What's this, cariad?" Dai asked as he entered the room.

"Oh, it's a statue," she replied casually. "The Joneses bought one for their bedroom. I liked it so much, I got one for us too." No more was said about the statue, not even later when they went to sleep. Around two in the morning, the husband got out of bed, went to the kitchen and returned a while later with a sandwich and a glass of milk.

"Here," he said to the statue, "eat something. I stood like an idiot at the Joneses' for three days, and nobody offered me as much as a glass of water."

x   x   x

Bronwen, Mari and Bethan, who work in the same office, notice that Mrs Johnson, their female boss, has started leaving work early every day, so one day they decide that after she leaves, they'll take off early, too. After all, she never calls or comes back, so how is she to know? Bronwen is thrilled to get home early. She does a little gardening, watches a bit of telly and then goes to bed early. Mari fach is elated, and does the shopping before going home to cook Dai's dinner. Bethan is also very happy to be home early, but as she goes upstairs she hears noises coming from her bedroom. She quietly opens the door a crack and is mortified to see her husband in bed with Mrs Johnson! Ever so gently, she closes the door and creeps out of her house.

The next day Bronwen and Mari talk about leaving early again, but when they ask Bethan if she wants to leave early also, she exclaims, "No way! Yesterday I almost got caught!"

x   x   x

Alan walks up to Megan in his office each day, stands very close to her, draws in a large breath of air and tells her that her hair smells nice. After a week of this, she can't stand it any longer. Megan goes to her supervisor and tells him what Alan is up to, and that she wants to file a sexual harassment complaint against him.

The supervisor is puzzled by this and asked, "What's sexually threatening about telling you that your hair smells nice?

Megan replies, "He's a ****ing dwarf!"

x   x   x

After the annual office party blow-out, Colin woke up with a pounding headache, cotton-mouthed, and utterly unable to recall the events of the preceding evening. After a trip to the bathroom, he was able to make his way downstairs, where his wife put some coffee in front of him.

"Bethan," he moaned, "Tell me what went on last night. Was it as bad as I think?"

"Even worse," she assured him, voice dripping with scorn. "You made a complete ass of yourself, succeeded in antagonizing the entire senior management and insulted the Regional Director to his face."

"He's an a**hole. I should have pissed on him."

"You did," Bethan informed him, "and he fired you."

"Well, screw him!" yelled Colin.

"I did!" said Bethan. "And you're back at work on Monday."

x x x

It was Owain's last day on the job after 35 years of carrying the post through all kinds of weather to the same village. When he arrived at the first house on his route, he was greeted by the whole family there, who all hugged and congratulated him and sent him on his way with a cheque for £25. At the second house they presented him with fine Cuban cigars in an 18-carat gold box. The folks at the third house handed him a case of 12-year-old Scotch whisky.

At the fourth house he was met at the door by a dumb blonde in her lingerie. She took him by the arm and led him up the stairs to the bedroom where she blew his mind with the most passionate love he had ever experienced. When he had enough they went downstairs, where the dumb blonde fixed him a giant breakfast: bacon, laverbread, eggs, tomatoes, beans, mushrooms, hash browns, black pudding, sausage, fried bread, toast and marmalade. When he was truly satisfied she poured him a mug of steaming tea. As she was pouring, he noticed a five pound note sticking out from under the mug's bottom edge.

"All this is just too wonderful for words," he said, "but what's the fiver for?"

"Well," said the dumb blonde, "last night I told my husband that today would be your last day, and that we should do something special for you. I asked him what to give you. He said, '***k him. Give him a fiver.' The breakfast was my idea."

Myfanwy walks up to Dai, who was wearing blue swimming trunks and says, "Dai, did you know your eyes match your bathers?" Dai replies, "Why? Are my eyes bulging?"

x  x  x

Three women are sitting in a doctor's office waiting for their pregnancy test results. Myfanwy says, "If I'm pregnant, it will be a girl, because I was on the bottom." Megan replies, "If I'm pregnant I will have a boy because I was on top." Mair thinks for a minute and says, "Then I'm going to have puppies!"

x  x  x

A couple of women were playing golf one sunny Saturday morning. The first of the twosome teed off and watched in horror as her ball headed directly toward a foursome of men playing the next hole.

Indeed, the ball hit one of the men, and he immediately clasped his hands together at his crotch, fell to the ground and proceeded to roll around in evident agony.

The woman rushed down to the man and immediately began to apologize. She said, "Please allow me to help. I'm a physical therapist and I know I could relieve your pain if you'd allow me."

"Ummph! Oooh! Nnooo... I'll be all right... I'll be fine in a few minutes," he replied breathlessly as he remained in the foetal position, still clasping his hands together at his crotch. But she persisted, and he finally allowed her to help him. She gently took his hands away and laid them to the side, loosened his pants, and put her hands inside. She began to massage him.

She then asked him, "How does that feel?"

To which he replied, "It feels great, but my thumb still hurts like hell."

# men XXX

Geraint joins a very exclusive nudist camp on Anglesey. On his first day, he takes off his clothes and starts wandering around. A gorgeous petite blonde passes him and he immediately gets an erection.

The woman notices his erection, comes over to him grinning sweetly and says: "Sir, did you call for me?" Geraint replied: "No, what do you mean?" She says: "You must be new here; let me explain. It's a rule here that if I give you an erection, it implies you called for me." Smiling, she then leads him to the side of a pool, lays down on a towel, eagerly pulls him to her and happily lets him have his wicked way with her.

Geraint continues exploring the facilities. He enters a sauna, sits down, and farts. Within a few seconds a huge, horribly corpulent, hairy man with a firm erection lumbers out of the steam towards him. The huge man says: "Sir, did you call for me?"

"No, what do you mean?"

"You must be new here; it is a rule that when you fart, it implies you called for me." The huge man then easily spins Geraint around, bends him over the bench and has his way with him.

Geraint rushes back to the colony office. He is

greeted by the smiling naked receptionist: "Can I help you?" Geraint says: "Here's your card and key back. You can keep the £100 joining fee."

"But sir, you've only been here a couple of hours; you only saw a small fraction of our facilities..."

Geraint replies: "Listen, miss. I am 52 years old; I get a hard-on twice a month, but I fart 15 times a day!"

x   x   x

It was Christmas and the judge was in a merry mood as he asked Ianto, the defendant, "What are you charged with?"

"Doing my Christmas shopping early, sir," replied Ianto.

"Well that's not a crime," said the judge. "How early were you doing this shopping?"

"Before the store opened," answered Ianto.

x   x   x

Twm went to the dentist to get his teeth checked. While he was sitting in the chair being examined, the dentist said to him, "Have you done oral sex lately, Twm?" Twm replied, "Why yes, I did this morning actually. How could you tell? Did you find a pubic hair stuck in my tooth?" The dentist says, "No, not quite. You've got some shit on the end of your nose, Twm!"

x   x   x

Gareth calls the psychiatrist at a mental hospital and asks who's in room 24.

"Nobody," comes the reply.

"Good," says Gareth, "I must have escaped!"

x x x

Meic and Dai were a couple of drinking butties who worked as airplane mechanics in Aberporth. One day the airport was fogged in, and they were stuck in the hangar with nothing to do. Meic said, "Bloody hell Dai, I wish we had something to drink!"

"Me too, old mate."

"You know, I've heard you can drink jet fuel and get a buzz. Fancy trying it?"

So they pour themselves a couple of glasses of high octane hooch and get completely smashed.

The next morning Meic wakes up and is surprised at how good he feels. In fact he feels great. No hangover, no bad side effects. Nothing.

Then the phone rings – it's Dai. Dai says, "Hey, how do you feel this morning?"

"I feel great. How about you?"

"I feel great, too. You don't have a hangover?"

"No, that jet fuel is great stuff – no hangover, nothing. We ought to do this more often."

"Yeah, well, there's just one thing..." says Dai.

"What's that?"

"Have you farted yet?"

"No."

"Well, don't, because I'm in Essex!"

x x x

Evan wakes up one morning to find a gorilla on his roof. So he looks in the yellow pages and sure enough, there's an ad for gorilla removers. He calls the number, and the gorilla remover says he'll be over in 30 minutes. The gorilla remover arrives, and gets out of his van. He's got a ladder, a baseball bat, a shotgun and a mean old pit bull.

"What are you going to do?" Evan asks.

"I'm going to put this ladder up against the roof, then I'm going to go up there and knock the gorilla off the roof with this baseball bat. When the gorilla falls off, the pit bull is trained to grab his balls and not let go. The gorilla will then be subdued enough for me to put him in the cage in the back of the van." He hands the shotgun to the homeowner.

"What's the shotgun for?" asks the concerned and confused Evan.

"If the gorilla knocks me off the roof, shoot the pit bull."

x   x   x

Iestyn, who lived in the hills above Pontrhydfendigaid, took his son Dafydd out shooting one day. When they came back later that day, Dafydd put his shotgun on the kitchen table and hurried to the toilet. He put the gun down so roughly that it opened and the cartridge from the gun fell out, and the shot spilled into the cawl his mam had prepared. No-one had noticed the incident, so Dafydd kept quiet.

Later that afternoon, his Mam served dinner as usual.

Later that night, Dafydd's little sister ran

downstairs saying, "Mammy, Mammy! I just peed little black balls like hundreds and thousands!"

"Did it hurt?" asked her mam.

"No," replied the little the girl.

"Okay, then don't worry about it," said her mam.

Then his small brother ran downstairs, "Mammy, Mammy! I just peed little black balls like hundreds and thousands!"

"Did it hurt?" she says.

"No." says the little boy.

"Okay, then don't worry about it," says the mother.

Later that evening, Iestyn rushes down the stairs with his pants down.

"Cariad, cariad, quick! I was just upstairs ready to go to the loo when I farted and I shot the dog!"

x   x   x

There was this man who was injured in a horrible accident. But the only permanent damage he suffered was the amputation of both of his ears. As a result of this unusual handicap, he was very self-conscious. Because of the accident, he received a large sum of money from the insurance company. It was always his dream to own his own business, and realised that with all this money, he now had the means to own one. So he went out and purchased a small – but expanding – computer firm. But he realized that he had no business knowledge at all, so he decided to employ someone to run the business. He picked out three top applicants, and interviewed each of them. The first interview went really well. He really liked Dai. His last question for this first candidate was, "Do you notice anything unusual about me?" Dai said, "Now that you mention it, you have no ears." The man got really upset and threw Dai out.

The second interview went even better than the first. This candidate, Evan, was much better than the first. Again, to conclude the interview, the man asked the same question again, "Do you notice anything unusual about me?" Evan noticed, like Dai had, "You have no ears." The man was really upset again, and threw this second candidate out.

Then came the third interview. The third candidate, Ianto, was even better than the second, the best of all of them. Almost certain that he wanted to hire Ianto, the man once again asked, "Do you notice anything unusual about me?" Ianto replied, "Yes, I bet you are wearing contact lenses." Surprised, the man then asked, "Wow! That's quite perceptive of you! How could you tell?" Ianto burst out laughing, and said, "You can't wear glasses if you don't have any ears!"

x   x   x

Twm, Ianto and Dai were on a trip to Egypt. One day, they came across a harem tent filled with over 100 beautiful women. They started getting friendly with all the women, when suddenly the Sheik came in.

"I am the master of all these women. No-one else can touch them except me. You three men must pay for what you have done today. You will be punished in a manner corresponding to your profession."

The sheik turns to Twm and asks him what he does for a living. "I'm a gamekeeper," he replied. "Then we will shoot your penis off!" said the sheik.

He then turned to Ianto and asked him what he did for a living. "I'm a fireman," said Ianto. "Then we will burn your penis off!" said the sheik.

Finally, he asked Dai, "And you, what do you do for a living?" And Dai answered, with a sly grin, "I'm a lollipop salesman!"

x x x

Wil, Twm and Ianto were working on a high-rise building project. Wil falls off and is killed instantly. As the ambulance takes the body away, Twm says, "Someone should go and tell his wife." Ianto says, "OK, I'm pretty good at that sensitive stuff, I'll do it." Two hours later, he comes back carrying a 6-pack. Twm says, "Where did you get that, Ianto?"

"Wil's wife gave it to me."

"That's unbelievable! You told the lady her husband was dead and she gave you the beer?" Ianto says, "Well not exactly. When she answered the door, I said to her, 'You must be Wil's widow'. She said, 'No, I'm not a widow.' And I said, 'Wanna bet me a six-pack?'"

x x x

"Doc, I think my son has gonorrhea," Dilwyn told his doctor on the phone.

"Okay, don't be hard on him. He's just a kid," the doctor soothed. "Get him in here right away and I'll take care of him."

"But Doc, I've been screwing the maid too, and

I've got the same symptoms he has."

"Then you come in with him, and I'll fix you both up." Replied the doctor.

"Well," Dilwyn admitted, "I think my wife now has it too."

"***k!" the Doctor roared. "That means we've all got it!"

x   x   x

Ifan, a strong, muscular farmer's son from Abergwili, was visiting Newport to attend a friend's wedding. Sitting at the bar at the reception, knocking back his seventh pint, he noticed a cracking blonde, whom he had also noticed during the wedding ceremony at the church. His eyes never left her until she was seated on the other side of the bar.

Ifan got up, slowly walked around the bar to where she was. In his best Welsh accent, he then bluntly asked if she wanted to "leave this dump" and go to his hotel room "just to get to, like, know each other a bit better".

The blonde rolled her eyes in disbelief, immediately responding with, "I'm afraid that my awareness of your proclivities regarding the esoteric aspects of sexual behavior precludes any such erotic confrontation."

Ifan looked at her in amazement, somewhat stunned. After several seconds of embarassed silence, he finaly admitted, "Huh? I don't get it!"

"Exactly!" she said as she got up, turned on her heel, and left, leaving him standing there in puzzlement.

x  x  x

Dai took up ventriloquism and started touring the clubs and stopped to entertain at a bar in a small town in northern England. He's going through his usual run of stupid Englishmen jokes, when a large Englishman in the fourth row stands on his chair and says, "I've heard just about enough of your English jokes! You Celtic breeds are all the same! What makes you think you can stereotype Englishmen that way? What does a person's geographical upbringing and attributes have to do with their worth as a human being?"

The ventriloquist looks on in amazement.

"It's guys like you who keep Englishmen like me from being respected at work and in our community," he continued, "and of reaching my full potential as a person because you and your kind continue to perpetuate discrimination against all English people... all in the name of humour."

Flustered, Dai begins to apologize. The Englishman interjects, "You stay out of this, mister. I'm talking to that little bastard on your knee!"

x  x  x

One of the regular foursome was sick, so a new member named George filled in. He was very good and pleasant company so they asked him to join them again the following Sunday.

"9.30 okay?" they asked George, to which he replied, "Fine, but I may be about ten minutes late. Wait for me."

The following Sunday George showed up right on time. Not only that, but he played left-handed and beat them.

They agreed to meet the following Sunday at 9.30. George again said, "Okay, but I may be about ten minutes late. Wait for me."

The next Sunday, there was George, punctual to the dot. This time he played right-handed and beat them again. "Okay, for 9.30 next Sunday?" one of the foursome asked.

George said, "Sure, if I'm ten minutes late…"

Another golfer jumped in. "Wait a minute. You always say you may be ten minutes late. But you're always right on time and you beat us whether you play right or left handed."

George said, "Well, that's true – I'm superstitious. If I wake up and my wife is sleeping on her right side, I play right-handed. If she's sleeping on her left side, I play left-handed."

"What if she's lying on her back?"

"That's when I'm ten minutes late!"

x   x   x

On a farm near Dolgellau lived a man and a woman and their three sons. Early one morning, the woman woke up, and while looking out of the window on to the pasture, she saw that the family's only cow was lying dead in the field. The situation looked hopeless to her. How could she possibly continue to feed her family now?

In a depressed state of mind, she hung herself. When her husband awoke to find his wife dead, as well as the cow, he too began to see the hopelessness of the situation, and he shot himself in the head.

Now the oldest son woke up to discover his parents dead – and the cow – and he decided to go down to the river and drown himself.

When he got to the river, he discovered a mermaid sitting on the bank. She said, "I've seen all, and know the reason for your despair. But if you will have sex with me five times in a row, I will restore your parents and the cow to you."

The son agreed to try, but after four times, he was simply unable to satisfy her again. So the mermaid drowned him in the river.

Next the second oldest son woke up. After discovering what had happened, he too decided to throw himself into the river. The mermaid said to him, "If you will have sex with me ten times in a row, I will make everything right." And while the son tried his best (seven times), it was not enough to satisfy the mermaid, so she drowned him in the river.

The youngest son woke up and saw his parents dead, the dead cow in the field, and his brothers gone. He decided that life was a hopeless prospect, and he went down to the river to throw himself in.

And there he also met the mermaid. "I have seen all that has happened, and I can make everything right if you will only have sex with me fifteen times in a row."

The young son replied, "Is that all? Why not twenty times in a row?"

The mermaid was somewhat taken aback by this request. Then he said, "Hell, why not twenty-five times in a row?" And even as she was reluctantly agreeing to his request, he said, "Why not THIRTY times in a row?"

Finally, she said, "Enough! Okay, if you will have sex with me thirty times in a row, then I will bring everybody back to perfect health." Then the young son asked, "Wait! How do I know that thirty times in a row won't kill you like it did the cow?"

x　x　x

Dai, an extremely rich man, and Ianto, a poor man have the same wedding anniversary. They're both at Cardiff shopping centre, shopping for their wives. Ianto says to Dai, "What'd you get your wife this year?"

"A BMW and a diamond ring."

"Why'd you get her both?" Ianto says.

"If she doesn't like the ring, she can take it back happy."

"That's fair enough," Ianto says.

"Well Ianto, what did you get your wife?" Dai says.

"A pair of slippers and a dildo."

"Why'd you get her a pair of slippers and a dildo?" Dai says.

"If she doesn't like the slippers, she can go ***k herself!"

x　x　x

There are three guys from Cwm Rhondda sitting at a table eating dinner. Ianto says, "I have to go to the toilet," and he comes back with his hand by his ear. The other two say, "Why is your hand by your ear?"

Ianto says, "I am receiving a phone call," and he sits down.

Ifan says, "I have to go to the toilet." He comes back looking at his hand. The others ask, "Why are you looking at your hand?" He says, "I am receiving an e-mail," and he sits down. Then Ephraim says, "I have to go to the toilet."

Ephraim comes out with toilet paper coming out of his trousers. Ianto says, "Why do you have toilet paper coming out of your trousers?" Ephraim replies, "I am receiving a fax."

x x x

Dafydd once told his son that if he wanted to live a long life, the secret was to sprinkle a little gunpowder on his cornflakes every morning. The son did this religiously, and lived to be 93.

When he died, he left 14 children, 28 grandchildren, 35 great-grandchildren, and a 15-foot hole in the wall of the crematorium.

x x x

Ceri was at the bar, deep in private thoughts of his own, when he turned to a woman just passing and said, "Pardon me miss, do you happen to have the time?" In a strident voice, she responded, "How dare you make such a proposition to me!"

Ceri, dumbstruck, felt really embarrassed and was uncomfortably aware that every pair of eyes in the place had turned in his direction. He mumbled, "I just asked for the time, miss!"

In an even louder voice, the woman shrieked, "I will call the police if you say another word!"

Grabbing his drink and embarrassed very nearly to death, Ceri hastened to the far end of the room and huddled at a table, holding his breath and wondering how soon he could sneak out the door.

Not more than half a minute later, the woman joined him. In a quiet voice, she said, "I'm terribly sorry to have embarrassed you, but I am a psychologist and I am studying the reaction of human beings to shocking statements."

Ceri stared at her for five seconds, then he leaned back and bellowed, "You'd do all that for me all night long for just two quid? What's that?... and you'd do it to every guy in this bar for another ten quid?!"

x  x  x

A farmer was out on his Welsh hillside farm tending his flock one day, when he saw a man drinking with a cupped hand from the stream which ran down from one of his fields.

Realising the danger, he shouted over to the man, "Paid â yfed yr dw ^r! Mae'n ych-a-fi." The man at the stream lifted his head and put a cupped hand to his ear, shrugged his shoulders at the farmer, and carried on drinking.

Realising the man at the stream couldn't hear him, the farmer moved closer.

"Paid, fachgen! Dw ^r ych-a-fi! Sheep crappio yn y dw ^r!"

Still the walker couldn't hear the farmer. Finally the farmer walked right up to the man at the stream and once again said "Dw ^r yn ych-a-fi! Dim drinkio!"

"I'm dreadfully sorry, my good man. I couldn't understand a word you said, dear boy!" said the man at the stream in a fine English accent.

"Oh, I see!" said the farmer. "I was just saying that if you use both hands, you can get more in."

x  x  x

A psychiatrist on his rounds in a mental hospital sees a couple of patients behaving rather strangely. The first man, Garmon, is sitting on the edge of his bed clutching an imaginary steering wheel and making loud train noises "Chooo-Chooo! Whoooo-Whooooo!"

"What are you doing?" asks the doctor.

"I'm taking a train down to Cardiff Central," replies Garmon.

Somewhat taken aback, but not to be put off, the doctor moves on to the next bed where he can see some very energetic activity going on underneath the covers. On pulling them back he finds Meurig totally naked face down into the mattress.

"And what are you doing?" asks the doctor, a little perplexed.

"Well," pants Meurig, "While Garmon's in Cardiff, I'm ****ing his wife!"

x  x  x

Dafydd and his father were visiting Cardiff. It was the first time for them both ever to leave their home in Caerwedros. They were amazed by almost everything they saw, but especially by two shiny silver walls that could move apart and back together again. Dafydd asked his father, "What is this, Dad?" The father, never having seen an lift, responded, "Dai bach, I've never seen anything like this in my life. I don't know what it is."

While Dafydd and his father were watching wide-eyed, an old lady in a wheelchair rolled up to the moving walls and pressed a button. The walls opened and the lady rolled between them into a small room. The walls closed and the boy and his father watched small circles of lights with numbers above the walls light up.

They continued to watch the circles light up in the reverse direction. The walls opened up again and a beautiful 24-year-old woman stepped out.

The father yells to his son, "Dai, hurry – go get your mother!"

x x x

A solicitor, a teacher, and a colliery worker were discussing the relative merits of having a wife or a mistress.

The solicitor says, "A mistress is better. If you have a wife and want a divorce, it causes all sorts of legal problems.

The teacher says, "It's better to have a wife because the sense of security lowers your stress and is good for your health."

The coalworker says, "You're both wrong. It's best to have both so that when the wife thinks you're with the mistress and the mistress thinks you're with your wife, you can play darts at the Lion."

x   x   x

Owain had been taken by his parents for his first visit to a nudist camp. He was surprised at the different sizes of the male organs, and mentioned it to his father. The father, being rather well endowed, explained that it was a measure of intelligence, the big ones being clever and the small ones being stupid. That afternoon the father was looking for his wife and asked Owain if he had seen his mother.

"I saw her about ten minutes ago. She was with a really stupid man, but he seemed to be getting cleverer every minute!"

x   x   x

An army major in the Welsh Guards is visiting sick soldiers. He goes up to one private and asks, "What's your problem, soldier?"

"Chronic syphilis, sir!" replies Ianto.

"What treatment are you getting?"

"Five minutes with the wire brush each day, sir!"

"What's your ambition?"

"To get back to the front lines, sir, and fight for the honour of Wales!"

"Good man!" says the Major. He goes to the next bed. "What's your problem, soldier?"

"Chronic piles, sir!" replied Ifan.

"What treatment are you getting?"

"Five minutes with the wire brush each day, sir!"

"What's your ambition?"

"To get back to the front lines, sir, and fight for the honour of the Welsh!"

"Good man!" says the Major. He goes to the next bed. "What's your problem, Soldier?"

"Chronic gum disease, sir!" replies Dafydd.

"What treatment are you getting?"

"Five minutes with the wire brush each day, sir!"

"What's your ambition?"

"To get to the front of the line and get the wire brush before the other two – sir!"

x   x   x

A farmer had three sons. One day Geraint, the oldest, came to him and said that since he was graduating from university, he would really like to get a car.

His father said, "Geraint, come here." He took him to the barn and pointed to the tractor and said, "This tractor is needed for the farm but I promise, as soon as it's paid for, we'll get you a car." Geraint was not too happy, but he was very understanding.

A week later, his second son, Gareth, approached him wanting a motorbike. "Well," the father said, "as soon as the tractor is paid for, we'll see about getting you a scooter."

Shortly after, his youngest son, Gary, was bugging him for a bike. Again, the father gave him the lecture about the tractor needing to be paid off first.

While leaving the barn, Gary bach, a little disgusted with his father's explanation, saw the cockerel doing its cockerel duty with one of the hens. He promptly went over and kicked the cockerel off the hen's back, mumbling to himself.

His dad asked, "Gary, now why would you do something like that? He didn't do anything to deserve that."

Gary replied, "Hey, nobody around here rides anything until that tractor gets paid off!"

x    x    x

A Welshman, Englishman and Scotsman were sitting in a bar in Sydney.

The view was fantastic, the beer excellent, and the food exceptional.

"But," said the Scotsman, "I still prefer the pubs back home. Why, in Glasgow there's a little bar called Catfish's. Now the landlord there goes out of his way for the locals so much that when you buy four drinks, he'll buy the fifth one for you."

"Well," said the Englishman, "at my local, the Red Lion, the barman there will buy your third drink after you buy the first two."

"Ha, that's nothing," said the Welshman. "Back home in Ponty, there's the Bridge Bar. Now the moment you set foot in the place they'll buy you a drink, then another. All the drinks you like. Then when you've had enough drinks, they'll take you upstairs and see that you get laid. All of this is on the house."

The Englishman and the Scotsman immediately pour scorn on the Welshman's claims, but he swears that it's true.

"Well," said the Englishman, "did this actually happen to you?"

"No, not me myself personally, no," said the Welshman. "But it did happen to my little sister!"

x    x    x

Twm and Dai, both rather elderly men, used to go to the park every morning, drink their flask of coffee and read the paper together. One day Twm says to his friend Dai, "If one of us should die, we must promise to come back and tell the other how it is in heaven. Several months later, Dai passed away suddenly. Twm continued to go to the park every morning, but it was just not the same. One morning, he heard a sound coming from behind a tree.

"Twm," he hears a whisper, "is that you?"

"Aye, it's me."

"Remember Twm, I promised to come back and tell you what it's like over here? Well, in short, it's heaven! I wake up every morning, have a fabulous vegetarian breakfast, shag all morning, have a lovely lunch, shag all afternoon, have a wonderful vegetarian dinner, and go to sleep."

"Wow!" Dai responds. "Is that what heaven is really like?"

"Heaven? I'm not in heaven, Dai. I"m a rabbit on Fforestfach common!"

x  x  x

Mari and Wil were making passionate love in Wil's delivery van – you know, shag pile carpets, big double mattress in the back, all that – when suddenly Mari, being a bit on the kinky side, yells out, "Oh Wil, whip me, whip me!" Wil, not wanting to pass up this unique opportunity, obviously did not have any whips on hand, but in a flash of inspiration, opens the window, snaps the aerial off the van and proceeds to whip Mari until they both collapse in sadomasochistic ecstasy.

About a week later, Mari notices that the marks left by the whipping session are starting to weep a bit so she goes to the doctor. The doctor takes one look at the wounds and asks, "Did you get these marks having sex?" Mari is a little embarrassed but admits that, yes, she did. Nodding his head knowingly the doctor exclaims, "I thought so, because in all my years of doctoring, you've got the worst case of van aerial disease that I've ever seen!"

x   x   x

Tony picks up a fat girl in a bar. He's been there all night drinking and now he just wants to get laid. An hour later, they're busy ****ing when he says, "Can we switch the light off?"

"Why, Tony?" she asks, "Are you shy?"

"No," he replies, "it's just that the light's burning my ass!"

x   x   x

Dilwyn goes to the family doctor and asks if he can have a vasectomy. The doctor asks him if he's discussed the matter with his family.

"Of course I have," replied Dai, "and they're all in favour 15 to 1!"

x   x   x

Dilwyn turned to Ianto and complained to him that he was rather concerned, because he'd received a letter from a man who said if he didn't stop seeing his wife, he'd break his legs.

"Well, Dilwyn," replied Ianto, "are you going to stop seeing her?"

"It's not as easy as that," replied Dilwyn. "He didn't sign the letter."

x  x  x

On wall in ladies' toilet in the White Lion: "My husband follows me everywhere." Written just below it: "I don't."

x  x  x

Geraint: What have you been doing with all the grocery money I gave you?
Nia: Turn sideways and look in the mirror.

x  x  x

After spending the night with a young, sexy, passionate woman, Dai rolled over, and pulled a cigarette from his pants. He searched for his matches. Unable to find them, he asked the girl if she had a light. "There might be some matches in the top drawer." He opened the drawer of the bedside table and found a box of matches sitting neatly on top of a framed picture of another man. Naturally, Dai began to worry. "Is this your husband?" he inquired nervously.

"No, silly," she replied, snuggling up to him.

"Your boyfriend then?" he asked.

"No, not at all," she said, nibbling away at his ear.

"Well, who is he then?" demanded Dai. Calmly the girl replied, "That's me before the operation."

x   x   x

Meirion came home early from work one day and found Ruth wearing only a G-string and high heel shoes, and the room was absolutely soaking.

"What the hell's happened?" he said. "The whole house is flooded!"

"I think the water bed has burst," explained Ruth. With that a man, completely undressed, floats by.

"Who the bloody hell is that?" asks Meirion angrily.

"I don't know," replies Ruth. "I think he must be a lifeguard."

x   x   x

Dilwyn, who was getting on a bit, was now in a nursing home, and was chatting up an old flame, Betty Wyn, and they agreed that their sex life was all but finished. Betty agreed to sit on the garden seat each evening with her hand on his penis. This went okay for one week, when suddenly, old Mari fach was sitting in her place. Betty Wyn said, "Oh, so now you have another woman. What has she got that I haven't?" Dilwyn grinned and said, "Parkinson's."

x   x   x

Ianto, by now a feeble old man is in his doctor's office having a check-up. The doctor finishes the check-up and says to Ianto, "So, you seem in fine health. Any problems?"

"Yes, Doc," Ianto slowly responded. "My sex drive is too high and I need it lowered."

This took the doctor quite by surprise. "You're 84 years old, and you're in fine health for a man of your age, and I know men half your age who would kill for a problem like that. So, why are you complaining?"

"Well," Ianto said, "I see all these sexy nurses at the home, and when I go for a walk, I see all these cute little cariads all around, so that's why I'm here, Doc. I want my sex drive lowered."

Still confused, the doctor said, "I would think that at your age, you wouldn't complain about a high sex drive."

"Doc," Ianto said, "You don't understand. I need my sex drive lowered from here," pointing to his head, "to here," pointing to between his legs.

x   x   x

Dai was bored out of his silly little mind in the bar of the White Lion and was looking to strike up a conversation. He turns to the landlord and says, "Hey, about those Conservatives in Parliament..."

"Stop, pal - I don't allow talk about politics in my bar!" interrupted the landlord. A few minutes later Dai starts again, "People say about the Pope ..."

"No religion talk, either," John cuts in.

Dai gives it one more try to break the boredom. "I thought the Scarlets would..."

"No sports talk. That's how fights start in bars!" John said.

"Look, how about sex. Can I talk to you about sex?"

"Sure, we can talk about that," replied John.

"Great. Go ***k yourself!"

x x x

Tom was a keen country lad who applied for a salesman's job at a large department store in Cardiff. The boss asked him, "Have you ever been a salesman before?"

"Yes," replied Tom, "I was a salesman in the country." The boss liked the cut of him and said, "Start tomorrow and I'll come and see you at the end of the day when we close up." The day was long, but finally 5 o'clock came around. The boss asked, "How many sales did you make today?"

"One," said Tom.

"Only one?" blurted the boss. "Most of my staff make 20 or 30 sales a day. How much was the sale worth?"

"One hundred and forty three thousand pounds," said Tom.

"How did you manage that?" asked the flabbergasted boss.

"Well," said Tom, "this man came in and I sold him a small fish hook, then a medium hook and finally a really large hook. Then I sold him a small fishing line, a medium one and a huge big one. I asked him where he was going fishing and he said down the Bay. I said he would probably need a boat, so I took him down to the boat department and sold him that twenty foot schooner with the twin engines. Then he said his Volkswagen probably wouldn't be able to pull it, so I took him to the car department and sold him the new

4x4 Toyota." The boss took two steps back and asked in astonishment, "You sold all that to a guy who came in for a fish hook?"

"No," answered Tom, "He came in originally to buy a box of Tampons for his wife and I said to him, 'Your weekend's ****ed. You may as well go fishing.'"

x   x   x

Two friends, Ianto and Geraint, were having a round of golf one fine day. Towards the end of the golf course, Ianto had hit his ball into the woods. Geraint laughed and poked fun, but then somehow managed to hit his ball into the woods, just a few yards beyond where Ianto has hit his. Ianto looked for a long time, getting angrier every minute. Finally, he found his ball in a patch of pretty yellow buttercups. Instead of just continuing the game, he took his club and thrashed every single buttercup in the patch, smashing the weeds to pieces.

All of a sudden, in a flash and puff of smoke, a little old woman appeared.

She said, "I'm Mother Nature! Ianto, do you know how long it took me to make those buttercups? Just for that, you won't have any butter for your popcorn the rest of your life... better still; you won't have any butter for your toast for the rest of your life... as a matter of fact, you won't have any butter for anything the rest of your life!"

Then, POOF!...she was gone. After Ianto got a hold of himself, he hollered for his friend, "Geraint! Geraint! Where are you?" Geraint yelled, "I hit my ball in these damn pussywillows!"

Ianto screamed back, "DON'T SWING! FOR GOD'S SAKE, DON'T SWING!"

x x x

The SAS, the Welch Regiment and the South Wales Police decide to go on a survival weekend in the Brecon Beackons together, to see who comes out on top. After some basic exercises, the trainer tells them their next objective is to go down to the woods and come back with a rabbit for tea.

First up are the SAS. They don their infra-red goggles, drop to the ground, and crawl into the woods in formation. Absolute silence for five minutes, followed by a single muffled shot. They emerge with a rabbit, shot cleanly through the forehead.

"Excellent," says the trainer.

Next, the Welch regiment. They finish their cans of lager and cover themselves with camouflage cream, fix bayonets and charge down to the woods, screaming at the top of their voices. For the next half hour the woods ring with the sound of machine guns, mortar bombs, hand grenades and blood curdling war cries. They emerge with the charred remains of a rabbit.

"A bit messy, but you got a result. Well done!" said the trainer.

Lastly, in go the South Wales Police. Walking slowly, hands behind their backs, whistling 'Dixon of Dock Green'. For the next few hours, the silence is only broken by the crackle of walkie talkies – "Sierra oscar lima, suspect heading straight for you," etc. After what seems like an eternity, they emerge with a squirrel in handcuffs.

"What the hell do you think you're doing?" asks the trainer. "Take this squirrel back and get me a rabbit, like I asked you to, five hours ago." So back they go. Minutes pass. Minutes turn to hours. Day turns to night. The next morning the trainer and the rest of the crew are awakened by the police holding the squirrel, now covered in bruises.

"Are you taking the piss?" asked the seriously irate trainer. The police team leader shoots a glance at the squirrel who squeaks, "Alright, alright I'm a ****ing rabbit!"

x    x    x

A depressed young woman from Swansea was so desperate that she decided to end her life by throwing herself into the sea. When she went down the docks, a handsome young sailor noticed her tears and took pity on her.

"Look, you've got a lot to live for," he said. "I'm off to America in the morning, and if you like, I can stow you away on my ship. I'll take good care of you and bring you food every day." Moving closer, he slipped his arm around her shoulder and added, "I'll keep you happy, and you'll keep me happy," he winked. The girl nodded. After all, what did she have to lose?

That night, the sailor brought her aboard and hid her in a lifeboat. From then on, every night he brought her three sandwiches and a piece of fruit and they made passionate love until dawn. Three weeks later during a routine search, the captain discovered her.

"What are you doing here?" the captain asked.

"I have an arrangement with one of the sailors,"

she explained. "He's taking me to America, and he's feeding me."

"What are you doing for him?" said the captain.

"He's screwing me," said the girl.

"He certainly is," replied the captain. "This is the Ilfracombe Ferry."

Ianto, Dilwyn and Dai are drinking in the Angel when a drunk comes in, staggers up to them, and points at Ianto, shouting, "Your mum's the best shag in town!" Everyone expects a fight, but Ianto ignores him, so the drunk wanders off and stick his nose into a pint of Brains at the far end of the bar.

Ten minutes later, the drunk comes back, points at Ianto again, and says, "I just screwed your mam, and it was great!" Again Ianto refuses to take the bait, and the drunk goes back to the far end of the bar.

Ten minutes later, he comes back and announces, "Your mam said it was the best thing since sliced bread!"

Finally Ianto interrupts. "Go home, Dad... you're pissed!"

x  x  x

# marriage XXX

Ianto walked up to a farmer's house, and knocked on the door. When the farmer's wife opened the door, the man asked if she knew how to have sex. Not amused, she slammed the door. Again, Ianto knocked, and again, he asked the same question. Again, she slammed the door and screamed, "Get the hell away!"

Later, she told her husband of the incident. He said he would stay home the following day just in case.

Sure enough, the next day, Ianto returned. The husband hid with his gun while his wife answered the door. When she was asked again if she knew how to have sex she said, "Yes!"

Ianto replied, "Great! Give some to your husband the next time you see him, and tell him to keep away from my wife!"

x   x   x

Ianto hobbled into his favorite pub on a crutch, one arm in plaster.

"My god! What happened to you?" the landlord asked.

"I got in a tiff with Mr Jones, Penuwch," whispered Ianto.

"Mr Jones Penuwch? He's just a wee fellow," the landlord said, surprised. "He must have had something in his hand."

"Aye, he did," Ianto said. "A shovel it was."

"Dear Lord! Didn't you have anything in your hand?"

"Aye, that I did – Mrs Jones's right tit," Ianto said. "And a beautiful thing it was, but not much use in a fight!"

x   x   x

Dai was driving home late one afternoon, over the speed limit. He noticed that a police car with its lights flashing in his rear mirror. He thinks he can outrun this cop, so he sticks his pedal to the metal and the race is on. The cars are racing down the A470 at 50, 60, 70, 80, 90 miles an hour. Finally, as his speedo crosses 100, Dai gives up. He pulls his car over to the lay-by. The police officer gets out of his car and approaches Dai. He leans down and says, "Listen mister, I've had a really bad day, and I just want to go home. Give me a good reason and I'll let you go." Dai thought for a moment and said, "Three weeks ago, my wife ran off with a police officer. When I saw your car in my rear mirror, I thought that you were the officer and that you were trying to give her back to me!" Dai got away with it.

x   x   x

In the middle of his honeymoon, Gareth, a young hillbilly bridegroom from Llanbrynmair, leaves his bride back at the hotel and shows up at his parents home, completely distraught. His dad asks him, "Gareth bach, why are you not with your bride on your honeymoon?"

"Dad, I was just getting ready to love my Mari when she told me she was a virgin. So I've come to ask what do I do."

"Boyo, don't tell me you didn't know what to do with her, especially a virgin."

"Dad, of course I know what to do with a woman, but Mari is now my wife."

"So what difference does this make?"

"Well, Dad, I just thought that if she isn't good enough for the boys, she isn't good enough for me!"

x  x  x

Ianto was sitting on the park bench with Wil, when he said. "Do you know Wil, for 25 years, Megan and myself were perfectly happy."

"Oh?" said Wil. "And what happened then?"

"We got married," replied Ianto.

x  x  x

Sam and Bessie are old age pensioners, and Sam always wanted an expensive pair of alligator cowboy boots for line dancing. Seeing some on sale one day, he buys a pair and wears them home, asking Bessie, "So, do you notice anything different about me?"

"What's different? It's the same shirt you wore yesterday and the same trousers. What's different?" Frustrated, Sam goes into the bathroom, undresses and comes out completely naked, wearing only his new boots. Again he says, "Bessie, do you notice anything different?"

"What's different, Sam? It's hanging down today;

it was hanging down yesterday and will be hanging down tomorrow." Angrily Sam yells, "Do you know why it's hanging down? Because it's looking at my new boots!"

Bessie replies, "You should have bought a hat!"

x x x

Ianto and Myfanwy were in the lounge one Saturday evening making love. During the session, Ianto said to Myfanwy, "Cariad, you're a bit dry tonight."

Myfanwy replied, "Ianto, for the past twenty minutes you've been licking the carpet!"

x x x

Ifor and Megan get married, and Ifor asks Megan if he can have a dresser drawer of his own that she will never open. Megan agrees. After 25 years of marriage, she notices that the drawer has been left open. She takes a quick look inside and sees three golf balls and about a £1,000 cash.

She confronts Ifor and asks for an explanation. He explains, "Every time I was unfaithful to you, I put a golf ball in the drawer." She calculated that three times in 25 years wasn't all that bad, as there had been very happy times, so she asked, "But what about the £1,000 cash?" Ifor answered, "Whenever I got a dozen golf balls, I sold them."

x x x

Dilwyn and Marian took on an 18-year-old girl, Myfanwy, as a lodger. She asked if she could have a bath. Marian said they didn't have a bathroom, but she could use a tin bath in front of the fire. "Monday's the best night, when Dilwyn goes out to play darts," she said, so Myfanwy agreed to have a bath the following Monday. After Dilwyn had gone to the pub for his darts match, Marian filled the bath and watched as Myfanwy got undressed. She was surprised to see that Myfanwy bach didn't have any pubic hair and told Dilwyn when he came home. Dilwyn didn't believe her so Marian said: "Next week I'll leave a gap in the curtains so that you can see for yourself."

The following Monday, while Myfanwy again got undressed, Marian asked : "Do you shave?"

"No," said the Myfanwy. "I've just never grown any hairs down there. Do you have hairs?"

"Oh yes," said Marian and she showed off her great, hairy muff. When Dilwyn got back in she asked: "Did you see?"

"Yes," he said. "But why the ***k did you have to show her yours?"

"Why?" she said. "You've seen it all before."

"I know," he said, "but the ***king darts team hadn't."

x  x  x

A woman in the bar says she wants to have plastic surgery to enlarge her breasts. Her husband Ianto tells her, "Hey, you don't need surgery to do that. I know how to do it without surgery."

Myfanwy asks, "How do I do it without surgery?"

"Just rub toilet paper between them."

Startled, Myfanwy asks, "How does that make them bigger?"

"I don't know, but it worked for your arse."

x x x

One day Blodwen met Seimon on the mountain above Plas Tan-y-Bwlch and was immediately very attracted to him and during her questions about his life she asked him how he managed for sex.

"What's that?" Seimon asked.

Blodwen explained to him what sex was and he said, "Oh, I use a hole in the trunk of a tree."

Horrified, she said, "Seimon, you have it all wrong, but I will show you how to do it properly." Blodwen took off her clothes, laid down on the ground, and spread her legs wide. "Here," she said, "you must put it in here."

Seimon removed his Y-fronts, stepped closer, and then gave her an almighty kick in the crotch.

Blodwen rolled around in agony. Eventually, she managed to gasp, "What the hell did you do that for?"

"Just checking for bees."

x x x

Huw and Megan had been married for 25 years. One afternoon, Megan was working in the garden while Huw was grilling sausages and steaks on the BBQ out on the lawn.

As Megan was bending over pulling weeds, Huw said... "Hey cariad, you're getting fat. Your bum is huge. I'll bet it's as wide as the grill on this BBQ." Feeling the need to prove his point, Huw got out a tape measure and measured the grill, then Megan's bum.

"Aye," he said, "just what I thought, just about the same size." Megan became mad and left him outside alone. She went inside the house and didn't speak to him for the rest of the day. Later, when they went to bed, Huw cuddled up to Megan and said, "How about it, cariad? How about a little how's-your-father?" Megan turned her back to him, giving him the cold shoulder.

"What's the matter?" he asked. Megan replied... "You don't think I'm going to fire up this big grill just for one little old sausage, do you?"

x x x

Ianto and Myfanwy had two stunningly beautiful blonde teenaged daughters. They decided to try one last time for the son they always wanted. After months of trying, Myfanwy became pregnant and sure enough, nine months later, delivered a healthy baby boy. Ianto rushed to the ward to see his new son. He took one look and was horrified to see the ugliest child he had ever seen. He went to Myfanwy and said that there was no way that he could be the father of that baby.

"Look at the two beautiful daughters I fathered." Then he gave her a stern look and asked, "Have you been playing around?"

Myfanwy just smiled sweetly and said, "Not this time, Ianto."

x x x

Dafydd: Why don't you tell me when you have an orgasm?
Heather: I would, but you're never there.

x x x

Dai and Mari fach were in their honeymoon suite on their wedding night. As they undressed for bed, Dai, who was a big burly valleys miner, tossed his underpants to Mari and said, "Here, put these on." She put them on and the waist was twice the size of her body.

"I can't wear your pants," she said.

"That's right," said Dai, "and don't forget it. I'm the man in this family." With that, Mari fach whipped him her panties and said to Dai, "Now you try these on." He tried them on and found he could only get them on as far as his kneecaps. Dai said, "Bloody hell, I can't get into your pants." Mari said, "That's right, and that's the way it's going to be until your damn attitude changes!"

x x x

Dai and Mari got married, and in their valley, it was tradition that the best man dance with the bride for the first song. Well, this happened... but Ianto and Mari then danced for the second song too, and the third. By the time the fourth song came on, Dai ran up and kicked Mari between the legs. A riot broke out, and all the invited guests were hauled off to jail.

In front of the beak the next week, the judge asked Ianto what happened.

"Your honour, we were just dancing, and Dai ran up and kicked Mari between the legs."

"That must have hurt," said the judge.

"No kidding," said Ianto. "I broke three of my fingers."

× × ×

Ianto and Marged had just been married and had gone to a hotel for their honeymoon. Ianto went to the front desk and asked for a room. He said this occasion was very special to them and they needed a good room. The receptionist asked if he wanted the bridal. Ianto thought about it a while and then replied, "No, I'll just hold onto Marged's ears until she gets used to it."

× × ×

A man comes home from work, thinking no-one else is home yet. As he puts down his briefcase and hat, he hears a faint moaning coming from his eldest daughter's bedroom. Not quite sure what's going on, he tiptoes down the hallway and gently pushes open the door, only to find his daughter on her back on her bed, eyes closed, using a dildo and on the verge of orgasm. Shocked, he blurts out, "What the hell do you think you're doing?" Visibly shaken, she quickly grabs a sheet to cover herself and yells at him to get out and close the door while she puts on some clothes.

Her father sits in the living room, appalled that

his beautiful daughter would pleasure herself in this manner. The daughter comes out and admonishes her dad for not knocking before entering, and then says, "Look — I'm 25 years old, I don't have a boyfriend, I've never had a boyfriend, and I probably never will have a boyfriend. But I have needs, and I have to take care of them, you know?" Her father says, "Listen — you just haven't had much luck with boyfriends. I'm sure you'll get one soon." She replies, "No, Dad. It's just not on the cards. I'll never ever get married. That's all. I'm sorry to disappoint you."

A few weeks later, the daughter comes home early one afternoon to find her father sitting on the living room couch, with a gin and tonic in one hand, and the dildo in his other hand, watching TV.

"Dad!" she yells out. "What in God's name are you doing?" The father casually looks over his shoulder at her and says, "What does it look like? I'm having a drink with my son-in-law."

x   x   x

Dai was having problems pleasing his wife with his premature ejaculation, so he went to see his doctor. The doctor tells Dai he'll do better in bed if he masturbates before having sex. Dai leaves, and on his way home he decides he'll have sex when he returns. So he finds a nice open spot on the side of the road and pulls over. He gets under the car, closes his eyes, and proceeds to 'check the axle' under his car. About five minutes later he feels a tug on his pants, and not wanting to see who it is, he asks, "Who is it?"

"It's the police — what do you think you're doing?" With his eyes still closed, Dai replies, "I'm checking my car's axle." The bobby says, "Well, you'd better check your brakes, too, because your car rolled down the hill five minutes ago."

x  x  x

Dr Jones had the reputation of helping couples increase the joy in their sex life, but always promised not to take a case if he felt he could not help them. The Davieses came to see the doctor, and he gave them thorough physical exams, psychological exams, and various tests and then concluded, "Yes, I am happy to say that I believe I can help you. On your way home from the surgery, stop at the grocery store and buy some grapes and some doughnuts. Go home, take off your clothes, and you, Mr Davies, roll the grapes across the floor until you make a bull's eye in Mrs Davies's love canal. Then on hands and knees you must crawl to her like a leopard and retrieve the grape using only your tongue. Then next, Mrs Davies, you must take the doughnuts and from across the room, toss them at Mr Davies until you make a ringer around his love pole. Then like a lioness, you must crawl to him and consume the doughnut."

The couple went home and their sex life became more and more wonderful. They told their friends, Mr and Mrs Williams that they should see Dr Jones.

Dr Jones greeted the Williamses and said he would not take the case unless he felt that he could help them; so he conducted the physical exams and the same battery of tests.

Then he told the Williamses the bad news. "I cannot help you, so I will not take your money. I believe your sex life is as good as it will ever be. I cannot help." Mr and Mrs Williams pleaded with him, and said, "You helped our friends Mr and Mrs Davies, now please, please help us."

"Well, all right," Dr Jones said. "On your way home from the surgery, stop at the grocery store and buy some oranges and a packet of Polos…"

x   x   x

A man had seven children and was very proud of his achievement. He was so proud of himself that he started calling his wife 'Mother of Seven' in spite of her objections.

One night they went to a party. The man decided that it was time to go home, and wanted to find out if his wife is ready to leave as well. He shouted at the top of his voice, "Shall we go home, Mother of Seven?" His wife, irritated by her husband's lack of discretion shouted back, "Anytime you're ready, Father of Four!"

x   x   x

A young couple left the sex therapist's office determined to develop more effective body language.

"Alright," said Dai, "when I want sex, I'll rub your right breast. When I don't want sex, I'll rub your left breast."

"Okay," said Myfanwy, "What should I do then?"

"Well, when you want to have sex," he told her,

"rub my penis once. When you don't want any sex, rub it 200 times."

x  x  x

Concerned about her relationship, a woman approaches her doctor and says, "Doc, I'm getting married this weekend and my fiancee thinks I'm a virgin. Is there anything you can do to help me?"

After the doctor stopped laughing, he says, "Medically, no, but here's something you can try. On the wedding night, when you're getting ready for bed, take an elastic band and slide it to your upper thigh. When your husband puts it in, snap the elastic band and tell him it's your virginity snapping."

The woman loves this idea, and knows her hubby-to-be will fall for this. They have a beautiful wedding and retire to the honeymoon suite. The wife gets ready for bed in the bathroom, slips the elastic band up her leg, finishes preparing and climbs into bed with her man.

Things begin to progress, and her hubby slips it in. She snaps the elastic band, and the hubby asks, "what the ***k was that? The wife explains, "Oh, nothing honey, that was just my virginity snapping."

The husband cries out, "Well, snap it again, it's got my balls!"

x  x  x

A young newlywed was telling his friend about his wedding night.

"Boy, was my girl dumb! She put a pillow under her ass instead of her head!"

x x x

Little Sion is passing his parents' bedroom in the middle of the night, in search of a glass of water. Hearing a lot of moaning and thumping, he peeks in and catches his folks in the act. Before dad can even react, little Sion exclaims "Oh, boy! Horsy ride! Daddy, can I ride on your back?"

Daddy, relieved that Sion's not asking more uncomfortable questions, and seeing the opportunity not to break his stride, agrees. Sion hops on and daddy starts going to town. Pretty soon mommy starts moaning and gasping.

Sion cries out "Hang on tight, Daddy! This is the part where me and the milkman usually get bucked off!"

x x x

Rhys walks in a bar and says to the barman, "Hey, Twm! Eight large whiskies and eight pints!"

Twm says, "Hell, what's the matter, Rhys bach?"

Rhys replied, "Well, my son has just come home from college and I found out he's gay."

Twm says, "Hey, Rhys that's terrible!" and gives Rhys his drinks.

Two weeks go by and Rhys again goes to the bar. He walks in and says, "Hey, Twm, eight large whiskies and eight pints?"

Twm says, "Well, bloody hell, Rhys, what's the matter this time?"

Rhys says, "Well, my other boy just come home from college and I found out that *he's* gay, too."

Twm says, "Rhys, that's a bloody shame," and gives him the the beer and whiskies.

Three weeks go by and Rhys again comes bursting through the doors and says, "Twm, I want every ****ing drink in the house!"

Twm says, "Bloody hell, doesn't anyone in your family love women?"

Rhys says, "Yeah, I just found out my wife does..."

# sheep XXX

Ap Hywel finally makes his fortune from Welsh cheese and is having his dream house bulit. As he talks to the architect on how he wants the house built he says, "See that oak tree there? Don't cut it down, because under that tree I made love for the first time."

The architect says he understands the sentimental value of the tree, and he will design the house so that the tree isn't harmed.

Then the man says, "And you see that tree over there? I don't want that cut either, because her mother stood there and watched as we made love."

The architect could hardly believe his ears, "That's incredible! What did her mother say?"

"Baaaaaa!"

x   x   x

Why did the Welsh bring back so many sheep from the Falkland Islands?
War brides.

x   x   x

A *Guardian* journalist had just arrived in an old Welsh village when he noticed a curious lack of women. Walking into the local pub he asked, "What do you do around here for entertainment?"

"Women, you mean?" he was asked. "There aren't none round here, butt. Round here folks \*\*\*k sheep."

"That's disgusting!" cried the journalist. "I've never heard of such moral degredation!"

However, after a few months, the journalist's rocks were beginning to ache and the sheep were looking more and more attractive. So he finally went out and found himself a comely sheep, brought her back to his room, shampooed her and then tied ribbons in her hair. After a bottle of champagne, he lured the sheep into his bedchamber and released his pent-up frustrations. Afterward, he escorted his four-legged lover to the pub for a drink. As the journalist and his woolly mate entered, a hush fell over the patrons and the anxious couple became the object of many stares.

"You bunch of bloody hypocrites!" the reporter yelled. "You've been \*\*\*\*ing sheep for years, but when I do it, you look at me like I'm some sort of crazy pervert!" One drinker at the back of the crowd spoke up, "Yes, but that's the policeman's girl!"

x   x   x

How do the Welsh find sheep in long grass? Quite good actually.

x   x   x

Sion Penuwch and Pero, his dog are shipwrecked onto a deserted island. After a few days he decides to look around the island. He discovers that the only other inhabitants are sheep. He recalls how his farm mates would brag how they would screw sheep for kicks and he says to himself: "I'll never be that desperate."

But a few days later he can't get those sheep out of his mind, and soon he's sneaking up on the flock. Just as he is about to pounce on a really cute one, Pero grabs his leg and won't let go. He snaps out of it, and thanks Pero for keeping him from making a fool of himself. This same scene happens every night for a month and soon Sion is really getting pissed off with Pero.

Suddenly one day, Sion spies a liferaft bobbing in the surf. In the raft is a beautiful young girl, half dead but still alive. He takes her back to his hut, revives her and nurses her back to health. After a few days the girl is feeling fine, and that evening a rush of gratitude sweeps over her. She confronts Sion: "I owe you my life. I'm yours forever. I'll do anything you want!"

"Anything?"

"Anything!!"

"OK, hold that dog for ten minutes!"

x   x   x

The Welsh Have invented a new use for sheep. Wool.

x   x   x

A young Cardiffian grew fed up with modern life and decided to leave the big city and become a shepherd in the Pumlumon hills, spending months in the seclusion of the mountains alone with his thoughts and sheep. He went up the high mountains where he found three older shepherds with a big flock of sheep, and asked them to show him the ropes. The shepherds agreed.

The young man spent a week with them. One evening by the fire he asked casually, "So how do you blokes get by with no women around here?" Said one of the men, "Why, with so many sheep around, who needs women?" The youngster shuddered: "Ych-a-fi! How horrible! How can you...?" The three men only smiled and said nothing.

Another week passed and one morning the young man realized that the tension in his groin had grown unbearable. He remembered what the men had said, and looking at the sheep, thought, "Hmm, why not after all...?" He chose a moment when none of the older shepherds were around, and grabbed one of the nearest sheep. However, the others showed up in a minute, and seeing him with the sheep burst out laughing.

"What? What?" shouted the young man, blushing. "You told me that's what you did yourselves, didn't you?"

"Yes, of course! But to choose the ugliest one?!"

x  x  x

Farmer Jones and his wife were lying in bed one evening; she was knitting, he was reading the latest issue of *Farmer's Weekly*. He looks up from the page and says to her, "Did you know that humans are the only species in which the female achieves orgasm?"

She looks at him wistfully, smiles, and replies, "Oh

yeah? Prove it."

He frowns for a moment, then says, "Okay." He then gets up and walks out, leaving his wife with a confused look on her face.

About a half an hour later, he returns all tired and sweaty and proclaims, "Well, I'm sure the cow and sheep didn't, but the way that pig's always squealing, how can I tell?"

x   x   x

Have you heard about the latest Welsh sex aid? Velcro gloves.

x   x   x

What do you call safe sex in Meirionydd? Marking an 'X' on the sheep that kick.

x   x   x

Driving along late one evening after playing a late-nighter in a lonely working men's club in Blaengarw, a ventriloquist's car broke down. Having walked along the road for a while, he came upon a small farmhouse on the moorland. Having explained his situation to the farmer who answered the traveller's knock, the farmer invited him in to spend the night. The farmer had no phone.

Inside the bleak farmhouse, the traveller was surprised to see no division between that part of it housing the human – the single old farmer – and the part housing the animals. Thinking there was some fun to be had, the traveller asked the farmer if he would mind if he talked to his horse, the farmer replied, "The horse doesn't talk."

The traveller waved at the farmer's horse, asking, "How's the old guy treating you then?" Throwing his voice, the ventriloquist answers, "Well, okay. He rides me pretty hard sometimes, but nothing that a little more hay wouldn't cure!"

The farmer stares in sheer amazement.

The traveller then looks at the collie slumbering on the mat in front of a sorry-looking fire and asks the farmer, "What sort of a day has your dog had, then?"

"The dog doesn't talk!" replied the farmer.

The traveller again throws his voice as if the dog were to say, "Can't complain really; a little more meat when he makes me gather sheep all day wouldn't go amiss though..."

The farmer's jaw drops lower...

The traveller now hears the bleating of an ewe somewhere in the dark corners of the barn beyond. He asks the farmer if he can go and have a chat with her, whereupon the farmer shoots to his feet and shouts.

"No bloody way! That ewe tells lies!"

x    x    x

What do you call a Welshman with more than one sheep?
A bigamist.

x    x    x

There was a typical north Wales blond called Anwen. She had long, blond hair, blue eyes, and she was sick of all the blond jokes. One day, she decided to get a make-over, so she cut and dyed her hair. She also went out and bought a new convertible. She went driving down a country road and came across a herd of sheep. She stopped and called the sheep herder over.

"That's a nice flock of sheep," She said.

"Well, thank you," Said the herder.

"Tell you what. I have a proposition for you," said the woman.

"Okay," Replied the herder.

"If I can guess the exact number of sheep in your flock, can I take one home?" asked Anwen.

"Certainly," said the sheep herder.

So, the girl sat up and looked at the herd for a second and then replied, "382."

"Wow!" said the herder. "That is exactly right. Go ahead and pick out the sheep you want to take home." So the woman went and picked one out and put it in her car. Then, the herder said, "Okay, now I have a proposition for you."

"What is it?" queried the woman.

"If I can guess the real colour of your hair, can I have my dog back?"

x  x  x

What do you get if you cross a sheep with a Border Collie?
A dog that rounds up Welshmen.

x   x   x

A missionary gets sent into deepest darkest Africa and goes to live with a tribe there. He spends years with the people, teaching them to read, write and the good Christian ways of the white man. One thing he particularly stresses is the evils of sexual sin. Thou must not commit adultery or fornication!

One day, the wife of one of the tribe's noblemen gives birth to a white child. The village is shocked and the chief is sent by his people to talk with the missionary. "You have taught us of the evils of sexual sin, yet here a black woman gives birth to a white child. You are the only white man that has ever set foot in our village. It doesn't take a genius to work out what has been going on!"

The missionary replies: "No, no, my good man. You are mistaken. What you have here is a natural occurence – what is called an albino. Look to thy yonder field. See a field of white sheep, and yet amongst them is one black one. Nature does this on occasion."

The chief pauses for a moment then says, "Tell you what, you don't say anything about the sheep, I won't say anything about the white child."

x   x   x

Why did God invent women?
Because he couldn't teach sheep to type!
And because sheep can't cook.

x   x   x

Two Welsh sheep drovers are sitting in their tent after a hard days work. Because of the size of the farm they work on, they are miles from home. They are both enjoying a bottle of mead under the shade of the awning of their tent when a man in a pin-striped suit, carrying a small brown briefcase and wearing a bowler hat passes by.

"Go and see who that bloody clown is, Arwyn; he must be lost," says the senior of the two. So Arwyn scampers off after the city type gent. After about fifty yards he catches him up.

"Scews me, boyo, are you lost or something?"

"Not at all, my man. I am conducting some field work connected with my employment," was the haughty reply.

"You must have a funny kind of job, bach. What do you do for a living?" said the drover.

"I am a taxidermist."

"No good you being out here then, boyos. There's no taxis out here."

"You don't understand. I stuff animals for a living."

The drover is bemused but eventually asks, "What sort of animals do you stuff?"

"Well, I've stuffed all sorts in my time, fish, birds, snakes, rabbits, crocodiles and I even stuffed an emu once."

The drover is now very suspicious: "You ever stuffed a sheep?"

"Why, certainly."

When the drover eventually returns to the tent his mate asks, "Well, who was that man?"

"Nobody special," was the reply, "just another drover."

x x x

What do the Welsh call a flock of sheep?
A Harem/Girl Friends/a good time etc...

x x x

A yuppie from the city of London takes his young family out for a day in the Welsh countryside, driving along, and the two angelic kiddies cried in an awfully upper class voice, "Daddy, Daddy, what is that strange beast?"

"That, my children is a cow."

More driving.

"Daddy, Daddy, What is that building?"

"That, my children is Castell y Bere."

"Daddy, Daddy, What is that man doing?"

"Well, I'm not exactly sure, my angels..."

"Oh, but Daddy, we want to know!" chorused the children.

So Daddy parks up, and calls down to a man, bent over a sheep.

"I say, Taffy, are you shearing that sheep?"

The woollyback replied, "What you saying there, mun?"

"I said, are you shearing that sheep?"

"No! Bugger off and find your own!"

x x x

What do you call a Welshman with 500 girlfriends?
A shepherd.

x x x

An English pilot named Sims and Welsh co-pilot named Jenkins are flying a four-engine transport aircraft across country hauling a load of sheep.

When one of the engines conks out, Jenkins gets nervous, but Sims manages to calm him. "We can still make it easily to our destination on three engines," he says.

An hour later a second engine falters and stops running. Jenkins is sweating now and getting more nervous.

"Calm down," Sims says. "We're at 30,000 feet. We can still reach our destination by entering a shallow dive." And Jenkins returns to normal.

An hour later a third engine ceases to function. Jenkins is nearly frantic, but Sims comes through again.

"We're very close to our destination now, and we still have plenty of altitude. I promise you we'll make it!" And Jenkins is okay again.

Fifteen minutes later they're down to 5,000 feet altitude, 75 miles short of their destination, and the last engine quits. Jenkins is in a frenzy of fear. And quite frankly, Sims is too. "We have to bail out," he says.

"But what about the sheep?!" Jenkins asks.

"***k the sheep!" Sims shouts.

"You mean we still have time?" Jenkins says.

x x x

Why then are there so many sheep in Wales?
Because God couldn't teach the Welsh to read.

x x x

Why do so many Welshmen marry English women?
Because sheep can't fetch beer from the fridge.

x x x

A Londoner visiting Snowdonia and a local shepherd were tending sheep in the mountains when they came across an ewe with her head caught in a fence.

The shepherd dropped his trousers, got down on his knees and had his way with the ewe. Satisfied, the shepherd buttoned up and turned to the Londoner.

"Fancy a go?" asked the shepherd.

"Don't mind if I do..." said the Londoner, so he drops his trousers, gets on his knees, and sticks his head in the fence...

# miscellany XXX

Two nuns were driving down the road at night when a vampire jumped out in front of their car, causing them to slam on the brakes. The nun in the driver's seat panics, turns to the other nun and says, "Quick, show him your cross." So the other nun hastily rolls down her window and yells, "Get off the bonnet, you ugly toothy bastard!"

x   x   x

It was the monthly meeting of Pwllheli Paranormal Society in the vestry of Bethania and the subject of that evening was ghosts. The reverend speaker got up and asked the audience whether any of them had had an intimate relationship with a ghost, and a small, wizened fellow at the back put up his hand, but said he didn't want to talk about it.

"Oh, come on – no need to be shy, fachgen," said the organiser, and after much coaxing the bloke came up to the stage.

"Now, ladies and gents, I'm delighted to say we have someone with us tonight who has had an intimate relationship with a ghost."

"What?!" gasped the man. "I thought you said 'goat'!"

x   x   x

A car was involved in an accident in a street. As expected, a large crowd gathered.

A newspaper reporter anxious to get the story could not get near the car. Being a clever sort, he started shouting loudly, "Let me through! Let me through! I am the son of the victim."

The crowd made way for him. Lying in front of the car was a donkey.

x x x

An older couple had a son, who was still living with them. The parents were a little worried, as the son was still unable to decide about his future career, so they decided to do a small test.

They took a fiver, a bible, and a bottle of whisky, and put them on the front hall table... then they hid, pretending they were not at home.

The father's plan was: "If our son takes the money, he will be a businessman, if he takes the bible, he will be a priest, but if he takes the bottle of whisky, I'm afraid our son will be a drunkard."

So the parents hid in the cwtsh-dan-stâr and waited nervously. Peeping through the keyhole they saw their son arrive. The son saw the fiver, looked at it against the light, and slipped it in his pocket. After that, he took the bible, flicked through it, and took it. Finally he grabbed the bottle, opened it, and took an appreciative whiff to be assured of the quality, then he left for his room, carrying all three items.

The father slapped his forehead, and said: "Heavens forbid, it's even worse than I could ever have imagined. Our son is going to be a politician!"

x x x

A doctor was addressing a large audience. "The material we put into our stomachs is enough to have killed most of us sitting here years ago," he said. "Red meat is awful! Soft drinks corrode your stomach lining. Chinese food is loaded with MSG. High-fat diets can be disastrous. And none of us realizes the long-term harm caused by the germs in our drinking water. But there is one thing that is the most dangerous of all and we all have, or will, eat it. Can anyone here tell me what food it is that causes the most grief and suffering for years after eating it?" After several seconds of quiet, Dai, an old man in the front row raises his hand and says, "Wedding cake."

x x x

A man walks up to the bar with an ostrich behind him. As he sits down, the barman comes over and asks for their order. The man says, "I'll have a pint." He turns to the ostrich and asks, "What's yours?"

"I'll have a pint, too," says the ostrich. The barman pulls the beer and says, "That will be £3.40, please."

The man reaches into his pocket and pulls out the exact change for payment. The next day, the man and the ostrich come in again, and the man says, "I'll have a pint," and the ostrich says, "I'll have the same." Once again the man reaches into his pocket and pays with the exact change. This becomes a routine until, late one evening, the two enter again.

"The usual?" asks the barman.

"Well, it's close to last orders, so I'll have a large

scotch," says the man.

"Same for me," says the ostrich.

"That will be £7.20," says the barman. Once again, the man pulls the exact change out of his pocket and places it on the bar. The barman can't hold back his curiosity any longer.

"Excuse me sir. How do you always manage to come up with the exact change out of your pocket every time?" the barman asks.

"Well," says the man, "several years ago I was cleaning the attic and found an old lamp. When I rubbed it a genie appeared and offered me two wishes. My first wish was that if I ever had to pay for anything, I just put my hand in my pocket, and the right amount of money will always be there."

"That's brilliant!" says the barman, "Most people would wish for a million pounds or something, but you'll always be as rich as you want for as long as you live!"

"That's right! Whether it's a gallon of milk or a Rolls Royce, the exact money is always there," says the man. The barman asks, "One other thing, sir, what's with the ostrich?"

"Oh, yes! My second wish was for a bird with long legs."

x  x  x

This man goes along to the Patent Office with some of his new designs. He says to the clerk, "I'd like to register my new invention. It's a folding bottle."

"Okay," says the clerk. "What do you call it?"

"A fottle," replies the inventor.

"A fottle? That's stupid! Can't you think of

something else?"

"I can think about it. I've got something else though. It's a folding carton."

"And what do you call that?" asks the clerk.

"A farton," replies the inventor.

"That's rude. You can't possibly call it that!"

"In that case," says the inventor, "you're really going to hate the name of my folding bucket!"

x   x   x

A man goes into hospital for a vasectomy.

Shortly after he recovers from his anaesthetic, his surgeon comes in and tells him: "Well, I've got good news and I've got bad news for you."

"Give me the bad news first, Doc," says the patient.

"I'm afraid that we accidentally cut your balls off during surgery, son."

"Oh my god!" the patient cries, breaking into tears.

"But the good news," the doctor adds, "is that we had them biopsied and you'll be relieved to know that they weren't malignant!"

x   x   x

George Bush met the Queen, and he turns round and says: "As I'm the President, I'm thinking of changing how my country is referred to, and I'm thinking that it should be a kingdom." The Queen replies, "I'm sorry Mr Bush, but to be a kingdom, you have to have a king in charge – and you're not a king."

George Bush thought a while and then said: "How about a principality, then?"

To which the Queen replied, "Again, to be a principality you have to be a prince – and you're not a prince."

Bush thought long and hard and came up with "How about an empire then?"

The Queen, getting a little annoyed by now, replies, "Look Bush, to be an empire you must have an emperor in charge – and you are not an emperor."

Before George Bush could utter another word, the Queen said: "I think you're doing quite nicely as a country."

x  x  x

Ianto and Mari were waiting at the hospital donation centre.

"What are you doing here today?" asks Ianto.

"Oh, I'm here to donate some blood. They're going to give me a cuppa for it," says Mari.

"Hmm, that's interesting," says Ianto. "I'm here to donate sperm, myself. But they pay me £10." Mari looked thoughtful for a moment, and they chatted some more before going their separate ways. Several months later, they met again in the donation centre.

"Oh, hi Mari!" says Ianto. "Here to donate blood again?"

"Unh unh," said Mari, shaking her head with her mouth closed.

x  x  x

A blonde and brunette were walking down the road. The brunette spots her husband, and he is carrying flowers. She says to the blonde, "Now I'm going to have to spread my legs!" The blonde says, "Why? Don't you have a vase?"

x x x

One night, while working behind the bar, Ceri, the barman notices this hideous looking fellow, really ugly, at the far end of the bar with several hot women around him. Finally, Ceri's curiosity gets the best of him, and he walks down to the ugly man. Ceri says, "Please don't get offended when I tell you this, but I couldn't help noticing you have several beautiful women hanging all over you, and, forgive me, but you are not exactly the most handsome person I've ever seen. In fact, you're quite ugly. Now, normally, I would think these ladies are attracted to you because of your money, but I can tell by the way you're dressed, and the fact that they're buying you drinks, it's not your money. So, tell me, sir, what is it about you that these women are so crazy about?"

The man paused a moment, smiled suggestively, licked his eyebrows, and said, "I haven't the foggiest idea."

x x x

Iorwerth goes to the doctor's and tells the receptionist that he's come for Mary Anne's test results. The receptionist says, "Oh, I'm sorry Iorwerth, there's been a problem. We have two sets of test results for a Mary Anne and we don't know which belongs to your wife. I'm afraid it's bad news or terrible news. One test shows Alzheimer's Disease, the other shows VD!"

"That's awful! What shall I do?"

"Well," replied the receptionist: "The doctor suggests you drop her off in the middle of Bridgend and if she finds her way home, don't ***k her."

x  x  x

There were three elderly men sitting in wheelchairs on the seafront at Clarach one sunny afternoon. They were ten years apart in age. One was 60, the other 70 and the last one 80 years old. The 60-year-old started complaining. He said, "I wish I could just piss all at once and not dribble, dribble, dribble all day and night."

The 70-year-old then said, "I don't have that problem. I just wish I could take one good dump and not ooze, ooze, ooze all day and night."

The 80-year-old started laughing at the other two. He said, "I don't have any of those problems. At 7.00 a.m. I take a good piss and at 9.00 a.m. I take a good shit. My only problem is that I don't wake up until noon!"

x  x  x

Iolo and Mari were in chapel. Iolo was sleeping and Mari was knitting. The preacher asked: "Who created the Earth and man?" Mari poked Iolo with her knitting needle, and Iolo screamed, "GOD!"

The preacher looked at him and said, "That's right." Then he asked, "Who is God's son?" Once more Mari poked Iolo with the needle, and he woke up and screamed, "Jesus Christ!"

Again, the preacher said, "Correct." Finally, the preacher asked, "What did Eve say to Adam, when she didn't want any more children?" Mari poked Iolo again, but this time he got up and screamed: "Poke me with that thing one more time and I'm going to rip it off!"

The preacher smiled and said, "That's right!"

x   x   x

There was this old priest from Merthyr who got sick of all the people in his parish who kept confessing to adultery. One Sunday, in the pulpit, he said, "If I hear one more person confess to adultery, I'll quit!" Well, everyone liked him, so they came up with a code word. Someone who had committed adultery would say they had "fallen." This seemed to satisfy the old priest and things went well, until he died at a ripe old age.

About a week after the new priest arrived, he visited the mayor of the town and seemed very concerned. The priest said, "You have to do something about the pavements in town. When people come into the confessional, they keep talking about having fallen." The mayor started to laugh, realizing that no-one had told the new priest about the code word. Before the mayor could explain, the priest shook an accusing finger at him and said, "I don't know what you're laughing about. Your wife fell three times this week."

x   x   x

The Pope is visiting a small town in the Rhondda and all the locals are dressed up in their Sunday best. Everyone lines up on main street hoping for a personal blessing from the Pope. Dai has put on his best suit and he's sure the Pope will stop and talk to him. He is standing next to a tramp who doesn't smell very good.

As the Pope comes walking by, he leans over and says something to the tramp and then walks right past Dai. He can't believe it, then it hits him. The Pope won't talk to him; he's concerned for the unfortunate people: the poor and and feeble ones.

Thinking fast, he gives the bum £20 to swop clothes with him. He puts on the tramp's clothes and runs down the street to line up for another chance for the Pope to stop and talk to him. Sure enough, the Pope walks right up to him this time, leans over close and snarls, "I thought I told you to ***k off out of here!"

x   x   x

Marc, out on the golf course, takes a high speed ball right in the crotch. Writhing in agony, he falls to the ground. When he finally gets himself to the doctor, he says, "How bad is it, Doc? I'm going on my honeymoon next week and my fiancee is still a virgin in every way."

The doctor said, "I'll have to put your penis in a splint to let it heal and keep it straight. It should be okay next week." So he took four tongue depressors and formed a neat little four-sided bandage, and wired it all together; an impressive work of art. Marc mentions none of this to his girl, marries, and on his honeymoon night in the Bay, she rips open her blouse to reveal a gorgeous set of breasts.

This was the first time Marc had seen them. She says, "You'll be the first – no-one has ever touched these breasts."

He whips down his pants and says, "Look at this! It's still in the CRATE!"

x　x　x

Dilwyn was playing golf at a very exclusive course in Harlech for the first time, and on the sixth hole he hit a hole in one. Jubilant, he walked down to the green and, just as he was taking his ball from the cup, up popped a small green man, a leprechaun.

"Sor," the leprechaun bowed politely and continued. "This is a very exclusive course, and being as it faces the Emerald Isle, it has everything, including the services of a leprechaun, and as you made a hole in one in the sixth hole, I will be delighted to grant you any wish your heart desires."

"Bloody hell," said Dilwyn in shock. But seeing the leprechaun waiting so patiently, he thought for a minute then admitted shyly that he did have a wish.

"I want to have a longer penis," he confided.

"Your wish is granted, sor," the leprechaun said and disappeared in a puff of green smoke down the hole. So Dilwyn headed back to join up with his friends, and as he walked he could feel his penis slowly growing. The golf game progressed and Dilwyn's penis kept getting longer and longer until it came out beneath his shorts and reached down below his knees.

"Hmmmm," Dilwyn thought, "maybe this wasn't such

a great idea after all." So he left his friends and went back to the sixth hole with a bucket of balls and began to shoot. Finally he hit a hole in one, and by the time he got down to the green, he had to hold his penis to keep it from dragging on the ground. But he managed to take the ball from the cup and sure enough, out popped the leprechaun.

"Sor, this is a very exclusive course," said the leprechaun bowing once again, "and it has everything including the services of a leprechaun... oh! It's you again. Well, what will it be this time?"

"Could you give me some platform shoes?" pleaded Dilwyn.

x   x   x

A woman from Aberystwyth is learning to play golf at Ynys Las. She has been teaching herself to play for more than three months, and she is really bad. She decides to consult a golf pro. When she sees the pro, she explains how bad she is and he tells her to go ahead and hit the ball. She does. The ball goes about 50 yards into the brush slicing to the right. The pro says to the woman, "I can see that you have a lot of problems. Your stance is bad, your head is all over the place, and the worst thing is that grip." When she asks what can be done to fix the situation, he suggests, "Grab the club gently, as if you were grabbing your husband's penis. When the feeling is right, go ahead and swing." She does just that and the ball goes off the tee perfectly straight for about 275 yards. The pro says to the woman, "That's unbelievable. I didn't think you would do that well.

But now on to the next problem. How do we get that golf club out of your mouth?"

x x x

Dilwyn comes to work speaking in a hoarse voice. Jack asks him what happened to his voice. He relates that he was playing golf, and sliced his ball out of bounds and into a pasture. However, he thought he could find his ball, and went to look for it. He saw a woman looking for her ball, too. As he passed a cow, he noticed that there was a golf ball stuck in the back end of the cow. Dilwyn lifted up the cow's tail and called out, "Hey lady, does this look like yours?" That's when she hit him in the throat with a 3 iron.

x x x

A paper bag goes to see his doctor to get his test results.

The doctor says, "Well, I'm afraid it's bad news. You're HIV positive."

The bag can't believe it! "How can I possibly be? I'm a paper bag!" The doctor says, "Have you ever had unprotected sex?" The bag replies, "No, of course not. I'm a paper bag."

"Well, have you ever shared a needle?" continues the doctor.

"Of course not," says the bag.

"Well," the doctor continues, "are you haemophiliac?"

"No – don't be daft, I'm a paper bag," says the patient.

"Well, there's only one explanation," says the doctor. "Your mother must be a carrier!"

x   x   x

A group of Penrhyndeudraeth golfers were approaching the first tee when they noticed a woman being given first aid. One of the golfers asked what had happened, and he was informed that the woman had been stung by a bee and was having a reaction.

"Where was she bitten?" he asked.

"Between the first and second hole," was the reply.

He then replied, "Wow! She must have been standing right over the hive."

x   x   x

It's Corporal Davies's first day at a new base in Saudi Arabia, and the company clerk is showing him around the camp. They tour the entire base and the clerk shows him around and points out every building of interest. At the end of the tour, Davies says, "What about that little stable over there? What's that for?"

"Well," says the clerk, and looks at the ground in embarrassment, "you may have noticed there aren't any women on the base. You see, we keep a camel in that stable, so that when the men get their urges, they can..."

Davies holds up his hand, shakes his head and cuts off the clerk mid-sentence.

"PLEASE! Say no more. I get the point."

Well, as you can imagine, after a few weeks on the base, Davies too felt the need for a woman, and so he found himself at the clerk's desk one Saturday afternoon.

"Tell me," Davies said in a whisper, looking over his shoulder to be sure no-one else could hear, "is the camel free this afternoon?" The clerk checks his appointment book and nods in the affirmative. "How about I book you in for noon?" Davies nods and walks away.

At 12.00 he makes his way to the stable, walks in, and gently closes the door behind him. He finds a small stepping stool nearby, moves it behind the camel, and climbs onto it. Then he lowers his trousers, and begins making love to the camel.

Just as he's nearing his peak, the door opens suddenly and Davies spins around in shock and embarrassment to see the clerk standing there with a big grin on his face. As Davies begins to yell for him to leave, the clerk interrupts him with a quizzical look on his face.

"Begging your pardon, Corporal, but wouldn't it have been simpler for you to just ride the camel into town to find a woman, like the other men do?"

x  x  x

A young lady from the city decided she wanted to get rich quick. So, she proceeded to find herself a rich 73-year-old man from the Valleys, planning to screw him to death on their wedding night.

The courtship and wedding went off without any problem, in spite of the half-century age difference. On the first night of her honeymoon, she got undressed, and waited for him to come out of the bathroom to come to bed. When he emerged, however, he had nothing on except a rubber to cover a twelve-inch erection, and he was carrying a pair of earplugs and a pair of noseplugs.

Fearing her plan had gone desperately amiss, she asked, "What are those for?"

The elderly gent replied, "There are just two things I can't stand... the sound of a woman screaming, and the smell of burning rubber!"

x   x   x

A woman answers the door to a market researcher.

"Good morning, madam, I'm doing some research for Vaseline. Do you use it at all in your household?"

"Oh yes, all the time. It's very good for cuts, grazes and burns."

"Do you use it for anything else?"

"Well... ahem... er... well... during... ahem... sex."

"Well, madam. I am astonished by your honesty. Out of all the people who have completed our research questionnaire, you are first to admit using it for sex. Would you mind explaining for me how you use it during sex?"

"Oh, why of course! It's quite simple, really... the first thing we do is close the door. Then we just smear it all over the bedroom doorknob. This way the kids can't get in."

x   x   x

A man limps into a pub with a cane and a crocodile. The barman stops him and says, "Hold on a second here – you can't bring that animal in here. They aren't allowed!"

"But my gator here does a really cool trick." The barman says "Well then, let's see!" So the man whips out his \*\*\*k and shoves it in the croc's mouth. He then takes his cane and starts bashing the gator in the head with it. A crowd gathers around and everyone is astonished when he pulls out his \*\*\*k without a single scratch. He looks around at the crowd and says, "Does anyone else want to try?" An old lady raises her hand and says, "Alright, but don't hit me with that stick."

x   x   x

Two cows standing next to each other in a field. Daisy says to Dolly, "I was artificially inseminated this morning."

"I don't believe you," said Dolly.

"It's true – no bull!"

x   x   x

This morning as I was buttoning my shirt, a button fell off. After that, I picked up my briefcase, and the handle fell off. Then I went to open the door, and the doorknob fell off. I went to get into my car, and the door handle came off in my hand. Now I'm afraid to piss.

x   x   x

Two weeks ago was my fiftieth birthday, and I wasn't feeling too happy that morning anyway. I had breakfast, knowing my wife would be pleasant and at least say "happy birthday," and I'd most probably have a present.

She didn't even say "good morning," let alone a "happy birthday." I thought, "Well, that's women for you. Perhaps the kids will remember."

They came in for breakfast and didn't say a thing.

When I went to work I felt pretty low and despondent. As I walked into my office, my secretary, Myfanwy, said, "Good morning, Mr Jones, Happy Birthday." I felt better immediately; someone had remembered my birthday.

I worked until lunchtime, then Myfanwy knocked on my door and said, "You know, it's such a beautiful day outside and it's your birthday, let's go out for a few drinks, just the both of us." I said, "Bloody hell, that's the best thing I've heard all day. Let's go."

We went to the Llew Gwyn, not the place where we normally went and then went out into the country to another little private place, and had a few more bevvies.

On the way back to the office, Myfanwy said, "You know, it's such a nice day, and we don't have to go back to the office, do we?" I said, "No, not really." Myfanwy then said, "Let's go back to my place." After arriving at her apartment she said, "Mr Jones, if you don't mind, I think I'll go into the bedroom and get into something more comfortable."

"Okay," I excitedly replied. She went into the bedroom and, in about five minutes, she came out carrying a big birthday cake, followed by my wife, children and dozens of our friends, all singing "Happy Birthday", and there on the couch I sat... starkers!

x  x  x

I took some friends out to the Ivy Bush for dinner last week, and I noticed a spoon in the shirt pocket of our waiter as he handed us the menus. It seemed a little odd, but I dismissed it as a random thing. Until the waiter came with water and tableware; he too, sported a spoon in his breast pocket. I looked around the room, and all the waiters and waitresses had spoons in their pockets. When our waiter returned to take our order, I just had to ask, "Why the spoons?"

"Well, it's like this, it is, see," he explained, "our parent company recently hired some consultants to review all our routines, and after months of statistical analyses, they concluded that our customers drop spoons on the floor 73% more often than any other piece of cutlery, see; at a frequency of three spoons per hour per table. By preparing all our staff for this contingency in advance, we can cut our trips to the kitchen down and save time, see... nearly 1.5 extra man-hours per shift."

Just as he concluded, a 'ch-ching' came from the table behind him, and he quickly replaced a fallen spoon with the one from his pocket.

"I'll grab another spoon the next time I'm in the kitchen, aye, instead of making a special trip," he proudly explained.

I was impressed. "Thanks. I had to ask."

"Not at all, butt," he answered, then continued to

take our orders.

As the members of my dinner party took their turns, my eyes darted back and forth from each person ordering and my menu. That's when, out of the corner of my eye, I spotted a thin, black thread protruding from our waiter's fly. Again, I dismissed it; yet I had to scan the room and, sure enough, there were other waiters with strings hanging out of their trousers.

My curiosity overrode discretion at this point, so before he could leave I had to ask, "Excuse me, but... what about that string?"

"Oh, yes," he began in a quieter tone. "Not many people are that observant. The consultants found we could save time in the men's room, too."

"How's that?" I asked.

"See, by tying a string to the end of our, er... selves, we can pull it out at the urinals literally hands-free and thereby eliminate the need to wash our hands, cutting time spent in the toilet by over 93%, see!"

"Oh, that makes sense," I said, but then thinking through the process, I asked, "Hey, wait a bit. If the string helps you pull it out, how do you get it back in?"

"Well," he whispered, "I dunno about the other fellows; but I use the spoon in my pocket, see!"

Also Available:

**WELSH JOKES**
**Dilwyn Phillips**
086243 619 2
£3.95

**CELTIC JOKES**
**Dilwyn Philips**
086243 685 0
£3.95

**WELSH VALLEYS HUMOUR**
**David Jandrell**
086243 736 9
£3.95

For a full list of our publications, ask for a copy of our free catalogue or browse our website

**www.ylolfa.com**

to order online

TALYBONT CEREDIGION CYMRU SY24 5AP
*e-bost* ylolfa@ylolfa.com
*gwefan* www.ylolfa.com
*ffôn* (01970) 832 304
*ffacs* 832 782